There Must Be Something More!

There Must Be Something More!

by
Sid Roth
with
Irene Harrell

Messianic Vision Press
P.O. Box 1918
Brunswick, GA 31521

There Must Be Something More!
ISBN #0-910267-01-4

PUBLISHED BY
Messianic Vision Press
P.O. Box 1918
Brunswick, GA 31521

TYPESET BY
MasterTouch Publications
P.O. Box 2035
Hyde Park, NY 12538

COVER DESIGN AND LAYOUT BY
Now You See it! graphics

EDITED BY
Robert C. DuVall

Printed in the United States of America.

To Joy

Contents

Chapter One

Death Sentence

My God! How had anyone been able to stand me? Why hadn't somebody killed me long before now? I didn't like the sudden blinding revelation that showed me to myself, the revelation that I, who had always thought I was so wonderful, was a total washout as a person. It sickened, it hurt, I wanted to deny it, but try as I might, I couldn't think of one justification for my life. There wasn't a single good, decent quality in me. Why was God letting me live?

Maybe He wasn't! The thought careened through my head, and I couldn't stop it. Maybe the flashing of my whole life before me was a prelude to its end—that very day.

But God! I'm not ready to die!

I drove aimlessly around the city for several hours going like an automaton through the mechanical motions of stopping for traffic signals, changing lanes, accelerating, slowing, thinking. . . .

As I considered the life I'd lived, really seeing myself for the first time, the evil that was in me seemed to swell larger and larger, until I feared I would burst with it. But why? Why had I been like that? Why had I never seen it until now? Was there any hope for me?

As the unanswerable questions swirled, I considered crashing my car into the fast-moving traffic to wipe out the awfulness of the past. But I was afraid. If I did that, maybe I would land in hell, stuck with the awfulness that was myself for an unending forever.

Unexplainably, I found myself parking in front of a big bookstore I had frequented in the past. As I entered the store, my feet took me automatically down the aisle to the new age section. There, a book with a blue jacket leaped out at me—*The Bible, the Supernatural, and the Jews* by McCandlish Phillips. I reached for it, it fell open in my hands, and I began to read:

> *If you would not thrust your hand into a snake pit, you should not permit yourself to be drawn into an involvement with one or another form of occultism, even in a tentative and experimental way, without knowing that it is possible for you to step over a threshold and past a door that will slam shut behind you as soon as you stand on the far side of it—slam shut so tight that nothing you can do can ever get that door open again so that you can get back out.*

Had the door already slammed shut on me because of my involvement with horoscopes, fortune-telling, and mind control? My heart was beating wildly as my eyes skipped through the pages a little further. There I read something even more terrifying:

> *The door that can never be opened again slams shut faster on a Jew than on a non-Jew.*

The author went on to say that this is true because every Jew, whether he knows it or not, is in a covenant relationship with God.

I felt beads of sweat popping out on my forehead. My throat was on fire. The gooseflesh of fear enveloped my whole body. But I couldn't put the book down.

I shoved some money across the counter to the check-out clerk and dashed back to my car, the book tightly clenched under my arm.

I wasn't even aware of driving to the apartment, just of suddenly arriving there, slamming out of the car, dashing through the lobby and into my room, torn with warring desires. Part of me wanted to devour the book, to read every word; another part of me wanted to rip it to shreds, to set it on fire—anything to get rid of it!

The page to which I opened named prominent Jews who had lost their lives because they had dabbled in the occult, opening the door to the supernatural through acid rock music, alcohol, marijuana, drugs, yoga, martial arts, meditation, channeling, seances, psychic healing, acupuncture, hypnotism, and mind expansion.

There was Brian Epstein, manager of the Beatles. Brian, a multi-millionaire at thirty, was a Jew. He had dabbled in the occult, and he had died of an overdose of drugs. I shuddered, thinking how close I had come to following in his footsteps exactly. Phillips said that entering the supernatural world is like stepping across a manhole cover when you enter it, but when you want out, the cover is conveniently missing. The only way out is straight down into the very bowels of hell.

But I didn't want to die! I wasn't ready to die!

O God, help me! Somebody, help me!

I had to get in touch with God! I had to tell Him how sorry I was. For everything.

But I didn't know how to get in touch with God, and I didn't know who could help me. My fortune-teller couldn't help me. The mind control people couldn't help me. They said there was no such thing as evil. My rabbi? He'd probably send me to a psychiatrist who would lock me up and throw the key away. My mother couldn't help me. She didn't know how to reach God either.

Panic stricken, I rushed out and ran to a jewelry store in the neighborhood. There I bought a mezuzah and hung it around my neck. Maybe that would show God that I belonged to Him. I telephoned Joy, my estranged wife.

"Pray for me," I pleaded. "Pray like you've never prayed before! Pray to your God for me! Ask Him to help me. *Please* ask Him to help me. Ask Him to spare my life!"

I let the phone fall from my hand, weeping in an agony of despair.

I could feel the fear building in me, a tangible thing, building toward a crescendo. When the crash came—and when it was over (would it ever be over? or was terror eternal?)—where would I be? Or would there be anything left of me to be anywhere?

A man under a death sentence, I put a Bible under my pillow, felt the mezuzah around my neck and crawled, trembling, into bed. Lying there on my back, rigid with terror, I cried out, "O God of Abraham, Isaac, and Jacob, whoever You are, if You're listening, please, please help me. Get me out of the mess I'm in. I don't want to wake up, ever, if life has to be like this!"

It wasn't much of a prayer, but it came from a broken, empty man.

Chapter Two

King Me!

The train was crowded with well-dressed travelers going from Washington to New York for the holidays. Overhead racks were jammed with brightly wrapped packages and folded-up overcoats. All the seats were filled, and some extra passengers perched on their suitcases in the aisle. As the streamliner plowed its way through the snowcovered countryside, a small blond-headed boy wrestled himself loose from his father's restraining grasp and threw himself down in the aisle, screaming at the top of his lungs, beating his feet in a tantrum staccato against the green-carpeted floor of the passenger coach.

"Waaah! I'm starving! Waaah! I want a hamburger! Waaah! I want a hamburger! Waaah!"

There was almost a rhythm to it, punctuated by the rapid clicking of the train wheels along the track. The boy's father glowered ferociously and started to get up from his seat, but his wife's firm grip on his coattail pulled him down, her voice hypnotically persuasive.

"Be patient, Jack. After all, he's just a child. When he's older, then we can reason with him, teach him the difference between right and wrong. Right now, he probably is hungry. It's been a whole hour since lunch."

The man gave a deep sigh of resignation and pulled his coat close around him. Grunting what must have been an assent, he stared straight ahead. His wife rummaged in her capacious pocketbook and came up with a handful of shiny coins. Edging her way into the aisle, she knelt beside the still kicking, still screaming child.

"Here you are, Sidney," she purred, showing him the money. "Come with me, and I'll get the hamburger for you."

He stopped his wailing, looked as if he might begin all over again, and demanded suspiciously, "Can I have lots of ketchup on it?"

"A whole bottleful if you want it." The woman smiled at him, smoothing his hair and helping him to his feet. There seemed in her a vibrant pride and no shame at all that the coach full of passengers, who had been dozing, reading, or engaged in quiet conversation, had stopped what they were doing to stare at the almost unreal melodrama taking place before them.

But the scene was real enough for all of the three participants. They had been through many similar scenes in the past.

I was the temper-tantrum child, and my mother was the epitome of indulgence, my secret weapon against my father and anyone else in the world who didn't want to let me have my own way.

There are other scenes vivid in my memory even today. I can see myself running around our dining-room table, making "Nyah, nyah, nyah" faces at my father, in hot pursuit with his belt. But my secret weapon was always there between us, running interference for me, and I was never caught. I never felt the belt I so richly deserved. If I had, it might have made a difference in my life. It might have kept me from the day when, as a physically grown-up young man, I crawled into bed too terrified to close my eyes, but so scared of the mess I had made of my life that I thought it would be best for me to go to sleep and never wake up.

It was bad enough that my mother always pampered me in everything, but when I was four years old, much of the world joined her in letting me have my own way.

It all began when suddenly, for no reason that anyone could see, I started limping. I wasn't even aware of it myself until one night when there was a card party in our home. I had gone to bed early, sleeping as usual in my parents' bedroom. I woke up about midnight, as I had intended, in order to have some of the party refreshments. Rubbing the sleep out of my eyes, I stumbled into the living room in my rumpled pajamas.

"What's the matter with Sidney that he's limping so bad?" I heard someone ask my mother.

"Limping? My Sidney?" Mom was plainly startled. She slammed her handful of cards face down on the table and shoved her chair back, lines of real concern etched on her face.

"Aw, he's just faking, Ceal," My father said. "Come on, it's your bet . . . ."

But my mother had to find out right then what was wrong with her darling boy.

"Walk across the room to me, Sid," she pleaded, stretching out her arms.

I was happy to oblige, seeing that limping was a way of getting even more attention than usual. But I overdid the demonstration, walking with such an exaggerated limp, grimacing with such obviously fake pain on my face, that everyone except Mom burst out laughing and turned their attention back to the game.

I consoled myself thinking of the food Mom would be bringing out in just a little while. She made the best corned beef and pastrami sandwiches in the world and she'd probably give me an extra one since everybody had laughed at me. I could always count on her to make things right.

In the days that followed, I continued to limp, even when I

wasn't thinking about it. My father kept telling me to stop faking, but Mom grew more and more concerned.

"Something's really wrong with Sidney, Jack," I heard her say to my father a few days later when he came home from his work as a government electrician.

"That limping business, you mean?" He squinted at me through the smoke curling up from his perpetually dangling cigarette. "Aw, the kid's just trying to get attention."

"Jack! I know it's something serious!" Mom yelled so loud that Dad didn't say anything more. He buried himself in the evening paper and she picked up the telephone to make an appointment with an orthopedic specialist.

There were lots of tests, x-rays and more x-rays. The diagnosis: Legg-Perthes disease of the right hip. The treatment: I would have to get the weight off my hip so it could heal.

"Poor Sidney," Mom said, and the rest of the world demonstrated their sympathy, too.

At first I reveled in my new importance and the excitement of being fitted with crutches, braces, and a built-up shoe. Everyone showered me with gifts, and relatives and neighbors waited on me hand and foot. Even my father gave me everything I wanted for a while. When I went to the movies, someone would stand up to give me the best seat; when I entered the Halloween costume contest, I won first prize, not because my cowboy outfit was better than anyone else's, but because of my crutches. People who didn't know me thought that I was brave and wonderful. But their thinking it didn't make it so, and I grew fatter, sassier, and more spoiled than before. If there had been a contest about it, I could easily have won first prize for being the most obnoxious child in the world.

By the time I was old enough to be enrolled in kindergarten in the Hebrew Academy in Washington, D.C., I was sold on the idea that being crippled entitled me to everything I wanted from everybody. It must have been a real relief to my teachers when the doctors decided in January of my first-grade year that crutches and braces weren't doing the job. I was still putting too much weight on my hip, they said, and I would have to be taken out of school and hospitalized so my leg could be put in traction. That didn't sound too terrible to me, having my foot taped up and weights put on it. Besides, being in the hospital ought to be good for lots of presents!

In the hospital, I was challenged by a whole new group of people to bend to my way. But I soon learned that the nurses had had some experience in dealing with spoiled brats, and before long they demonstrated that they knew how to handle me.

A boy in the bed next to mine got to be my good friend, and we liked to trade our comic books and toys with one another. Since neither of us could get out of bed we buzzed for the nurses continually and asked them to make the exchanges for us. One day, a nurse had had enough. She explained that she was very busy taking care of other patients and that we should not buzz for her again unless we really needed her. Naturally, after that, we buzzed twice as often as before. We didn't know that the nurse had a secret weapon of her own.

The next morning, two green-coated interns, their surgical masks dangling around their necks, came into our room, rolling a stretcher.

"Is this the kid to be operated on?" one asked the other, jerking his head in my direction.

The other intern nodded gravely. Unsmiling, they began to maneuver the stretcher close to my bed. Their exceedingly serious manner unnerved me. Maybe they were going to cut my leg off!

"No!" I screamed as loud as I could. "Not me! It's a terrible mistake! Call my mother! Call my mother!"

I rolled to the far side of my bed kicking and screaming louder and louder until the interns left the room, taking the stretcher with them.

I was too scared to buzz the nurses for anything else the rest of that day. When my mother came to see me before bedtime, I told her what had happened, embellishing the truth with all the gory fictional detail my imagination could dream up. She listened in horror, her eyebrows climbing higher and higher, first in shock, then in super-righteous indignation.

Armed with my account of incredible sadistic torture, Mom rushed to the administrator's office and demanded that the two interns be fired, threatening a congressional investigation of the whole hospital staff.

I don't know what the administrator told her, but I do remember that I was transferred to a different hospital the next day. It was another case of my secret weapon at work, another case of my refusal to learn to behave in ways acceptable to the world.

When I was released from the second hospital, a visiting teacher came to my home to instruct me in what I had missed in school. Later, I was enrolled in a special health school with other handicapped children.

Chapter Three

Liar, Cheat

After I had spent three years in the health school, the doctors were satisfied that I was healed of the Legg-Perthes symptoms. They said I could discard my crutches and go to a regular public school with normal children. I was so excited about not being a cripple anymore that I was *almost* glad *not* to need special attention. But I got it anyway. My mother saw to that. She told the teacher that I had been a cripple, and the teacher explained it to the class and urged the boys and girls to be extra patient and kind to me. For a while, everyone cooperated, making it easy for me not to grow up.

Eventually, after the school kids got over the novelty of the fact that I had been a cripple, they began to tease me about how fat I was, that I couldn't run very fast, and that I was making near-failing grades in school.

I coped with their criticism in my own way. "I'm not fat," I assured myself. "Mom always says I'm handsome, so I can't be too fat." Satisfied about that, I kept on stuffing myself continually.

I justified myself in physical education class by telling anyone who would listen, "Even though I've been on crutches for a long time, I can still run faster than so-and-so." (We had one *really slow* boy in our class.)

But even I had to admit that my grades were terrible. I had become so lazy in my study habits in the health school, where many of the children had low-normal IQs, I began to think that maybe I *was* dumb. But I never admitted that to anyone, and I persuaded my mother that it was the teachers and the school who were dumb, instead. The next year, Mom put me in a private school where I would get more individual attention.

That didn't help. It actually made things worse. I was put in a class with poor and problem students, kids with learning disabilities. I was so far ahead of them at first that I just coasted for a while. By the time I realized that I was falling behind again, it was too late to catch up. Once again, I complained to my parents about what a stupid school I was in, and they put me back in public school the next year.

When things didn't go well for me in school, I was never reluctant to bring out my secret weapon. One day, a couple of boys teased me a little and shoved me. They were bigger and tougher than I was, so I didn't say anything at the time, but I vowed to get even with them. When I got home, I faked my way through a weepy scene with Mom, telling her how two big bullies had beaten me up.

The next morning, Mom was at school, and the teacher let me stand at the front of the classroom and point out the culprits so they could be taken to the principal's office for discipline. Then Mom passed out candy to the rest of the class, trying to buy their friendship for me.

Another time, I noticed that one of the boys in printing class had a better tray of print than I did. In my tray, the letters were all mixed up and I had to straighten them before I could set my type. In the other boy's tray, all the A's were in the right compartment, all the B's, and the rest of the alphabet was in order, too.

"It's because his brother went to school there," I whined, telling Mom about it when I got home. "And his brother was so smart.

That's why he got a better tray than me." She listened, full of sympathy, as always, and then she was on the phone, calling my classmate.

"You think you're so smart because your brother was a good student, and so you got the best tray, and my Sidney—" On and on she went, berating him, threatening him.

Sometimes I would be ashamed, but down deep inside, I must have wanted Mom to keep on fighting my battles for me, because I kept on tattling to her every time anything went wrong.

I had so much trouble adjusting to people in life, that my mother finally sent me to a counselor to see if he could help me work out my problems with people. I went to see him a number of times before he finally gave up on me because I refused to admit that anything was wrong—with me. I told him that I didn't have any problems that I knew of. The problems were in the other people, I assured him. And so the problems continued, the battles grew more fierce.

My battles weren't confined to the schoolroom, either. One day I got into an argument with the son of one of our roomers, and I picked up a knife and held it to his throat. When he told his widowed mother about it, she consulted a lawyer. Then she made a bad mistake. She reported the incident to my mom and told her that she was thinking of pressing charges against me. Mom's reaction was not at all what she expected.

"Out!" Mom screamed at her. "Not tomorrow, not tonight, but right this minute!" The whole neighborhood could hear her screaming "Out of this house you and your good-for-nothing son. I'm looking at the clock! Out! Out! How dare you!"

Mom was screaming, and the poor widow was practically on her knees asking Mom to forgive her, and asking me to forgive her and her son.

If there'd been an ounce of decency in me, I'd have felt sorry for them. But an ounce of decency, an iota of consideration for another human being, would have been lonesome in me.

In high school, I learned how to cheat in order to make the grades I wanted to have. I was good at cheating, and my eyes were always open to find new angles. One day in geometry class, I noticed that the teacher was copying our test onto the blackboard from a printed book of tests. Later that day, one of my friends told me that if I wanted to, I could probably buy a copy of the test book for myself with all the right answers printed in it! After school, I called the bookstore he suggested and sent my mother to buy the book for me. When she got home, I copied the answers for the next test we were supposed to have on a little slip of paper. At test time, I let it lie unobtrusively on the corner of my desk. I thought I was really cool to be writing the answers on my paper before the teacher even finished writing the problems on the board.

Even more fun than getting an A on the test was bragging to the other kids about how I was outsmarting the teacher. I thought I was outsmarting the teacher, too, when I let my friend Arnold copy my English homework every day for a whole semester. I thought we were getting by with it. But at the end of the semester, much to my surprise, the teacher held up before the class a couple of my homework papers and a couple of Arnold's.

"Isn't it interesting," she said, "that all semester long Sidney's papers and Arnold's have been identical? Now, Arnold and Sidney, I'm not going to ask who's cheating from whom. The one who copies work and the one who lets him copy it are both guilty. One's no better than the other." I could feel a sudden wave of heat spreading across my face, and I knew that even my ears were turning red with embarrassment. I shot Arnold a hate-filled look. *Why doesn't he at least tell her that he cheated from me?* I fumed. *The lousy cheat!* But I continued to cheat time and time again.

Once, I even cheated on a musical aptitude test!

I had studied, briefly, several instruments such as the piano, drum, guitar, clarinet, and trumpet but I didn't stick with any one instrument for more than a month, never long enough to learn anything. I was bored with having to spend time practicing scales and learning the rudiments. There was no glory, no public acclaim in that. I wanted to begin playing well immediately, and when I saw that mastering a particular instrument would take a lot of work, I dropped it and went on to something that looked easier.

When I was taking the aptitude test, I knew that the boy seated on my right had terrific musical ability, so I simply copied all his answers onto my paper.

When the test results were made known, my name was one of the two at the top of the list.

"These children have tremendous musical ability," the judge announced. I beamed back at him, adding another counterfeit star to my tarnished crown.

How I loved the glamour of recognition! How I despised the labor that led to real achievement! Somewhere in the deep recesses of my being, there was beginning to stir an awareness that my deviousness might catch up with me some day, but I shoved the awareness down and kept on my selfish way.

Two goals for my life were beginning to crystallize in my thinking about this time. The first, to have the acclaim of the world; the second, to make a million dollars. I dedicated myself to doing whatever I had to do to achieve these goals.

Chapter Four

Hypocrite, Sluggard

I arrived at a major milestone in my journey to fame and wealth on September 7, 1953.

"Clothes really make the man, Sidney. You look absolutely handsome in your tuxedo." My mother sighed proudly as she pinned a fresh carnation to my lapel. She had on a long lace and chiffon dress, her shoulder weighted with an elaborate corsage. Everybody was dressed up. There were gifts, money, and parties in my honor. My head was spinning with the excitement of my bar mitzvah, the celebration of my thirteenth birthday, the day when a Jewish boy becomes a man.

I had been preparing for this day for five years under a rabbi who was my special bar mitzvah instructor. I studied Hebrew, learned melodies to chant, memorized selections from my Haftorah, and practiced the speech I would make in English.

The day was supposed to have real spiritual significance for me. It marked my coming of age as a son of the commandments. Now I was responsible for keeping them. But I don't remember even so much as thinking about God on that day. My thoughts were entirely of myself and my day, my appearance, my presents, my fun.

In my home, we had always observed the Jewish holidays, usually making the trip to New York to spend them with my paternal grandparents. Those "vacations" had always been painful experiences for me. I disliked the long ride in the car or on a crowded train; climbing to the sixth floor of a tenement where there were no elevators; walking through the dark corridors that reeked with the stale aromas of food; boring hours sitting in the synagogue listening to a language I didn't understand; enduring interminable rituals that had no meaning or significance; all the relatives planting their sloppy kisses on me and asking stupid questions like, "How are you doing in school?" and "Sidney, you remember your uncle so-and-so?"

At these tribal gatherings, my parents were always bugging me. "Sidney, shake hands with your cousin. Sidney, did you say hello?" I always said hello, but I said it so softly that no one could hear me, and my father would keep after me, growing more and more exasperated, "Sidney, you didn't say hello!" Today, as I look back, I know that my father loved me and was only trying to bring me up right, but at that time, I took a perverse kind of delight in provoking him to the verge of apoplexy.

In the midst of the frustration, there were a few fun things I looked forward to—the seltzer water that sprayed from a nozzle, the matzo ball soup, the potato kugel, and getting a reward for the return of the matzo.

Stealing the piece of matzo, the unleavened bread, from under the pillow my grandfather sat on was my important part of the Passover seder, and the ceremony could not end until the matzo was back in grandfather's possession. It was part of the tradition that I was expected to demand a sum of money or a gift for its return.

One year, I fell asleep while the Passover seder was still going on. The prayers and Scripture readings always lasted for hours. Toward the end, my Uncle Willie woke me and handed me the matzo he had stolen for me. As I was thinking what gift I should ask for, or how much money I should demand, I made the smart-aleck mistake of waving the piece of matzo in front of my grandfather's face. With lightning speed, he grabbed it from my hand. I learned a new rule that holiday: never wave the matzo close to grandfather.

Although I didn't like everything about the holidays, and understood very little of their real significance, I was somehow, strangely, proud of my Jewishness. I knew I was born a Jew, would die a Jew, and knew with a fierce certainty that I would fight anyone who made fun of the Jews.

But attendance at the synagogue was another matter entirely. The only reason I went to the orthodox synagogue with my father was because I had to. The form of worship left me cold. There wasn't anything I liked about it except when we had refreshments.

I believed that there was a God, but the rabbi described God as a fire. What good could that kind of a God do for me?

It was all irrelevant, distant, and abstract. I couldn't understand Hebrew, and the cantor's chanting was totally meaningless to me. Besides all that, the hypocrisy really got to me.

For instance, we would always park our car two blocks from the synagogue so no one would know that we drove on the holidays. But most of the others parked there too, for the same reason. Once I happened to wave the car keys in the synagogue. My father's look almost drove me through the floor. I had utterly disgraced him.

Another time, my yarmulke, my little skull cap, fell off my head in the synagogue and onto the floor. I hadn't noticed it, but my father had.

"Where's the yarmulke?" he growled at me.

I put my hand to my head, felt that the cap was gone, and reached down to pick it up off the floor. My father was almost sick with disgust at me for having my head uncovered in the synagogue. A friend who was standing on the other side of him tried to calm him down.

"It's all right, Jack," he said, putting his hand on Dad's shoulder. "So the boy made a little mistake. Leave him alone already." I was so nervous I could hardly get my yarmulke back in place. Was it really such a sin to have my head uncovered?

And why did my relatives and friends smoke on high holy days when we were a block away from the synagogue where no one could see them, and then, when they got to the synagogue, why did they pretend they were abstaining from smoking? On high holy days, no one was supposed to light a fire for any purpose, because lighting a fire is work.

Why all the hypocrisy? Why?

I used to ask people about some of these things that bothered me, but everyone shrugged their shoulders and said nothing, as if they didn't know either. No one ever gave me a real answer.

The hypocrisy I observed in some orthodox Jews, the radical inconsistency between what they taught and how they lived, probably helped me to rationalize the dishonesty and the hypocrisy in my own life.

After my bar mitzvah, I didn't attend the synagogue anymore—except on holidays—until much later when I found out what the synagogue was really all about. But that was after I had been to hell and back.

My very first job on my way to winning the acclaim of the world and making a million dollars was as a paperboy in our neighborhood.

When I was in junior high, it seemed that almost every newspaper I picked up had a front-page picture of a paperboy grinning out at me. The write-up would tell how great they were, and paperboys were always winning prizes and going on trips to exciting places. Another definite drawing card, as far as I was concerned, was a promotional scheme in which, for every new subscriber, paperboys were given coupons redeemable with the Good Humor man. The thought of free ice cream treats was an irresistible come-on, and I nagged my parents until they agreed to sign the official documents that embarked me on my first business enterprise.

I delivered papers proudly for a few days, and got my parents, an uncle, and a few close neighbors as new subscribers. Then I woke up to a morning when it was pouring rain outside. I was so cozy and warm in bed, that instead of getting up to deliver the papers in the rain, I manufactured a sudden terrible cold, coughing so violently that my mother and sister brought me cough syrup and a hot-water bottle and insisted on delivering my papers for me while I stayed in bed and read the comic strips. That was so enjoyable that I had many fake sick days after that, days when it was sunny as well as when it rained, and the papers got delivered by my mom and my sister Shirley. If they ever caught on to my game, they never mentioned it. I, of course, was the one who got to pocket the profits.

After I got too big and important to work as a mere paper boy, I went to work running errands for my Uncle Abe, who owned a watch repair shop. I liked my uncle and thought it would be fun going to drug stores and variety stores that took in watches to repair, delivering them to my uncle so he could fix them, and then taking them back to the stores again.

For two weeks, I got along fine. I enjoyed the prestige of carrying valuable merchandise around the city. But late one afternoon, when there were no pickups to be made, no watches ready for delivery, my uncle handed me a can of scouring powder and a rag.

"Here, Sidney," he said, "the workroom sink looks terrible today. Give it a good scouring for me."

I couldn't believe my ears. Me? Scour a sink? I looked at the grimy sink, appalled that he would ask me to do such a menial, low-grade job. Why, anybody could clean a sink. It was beneath my dignity as a messenger delivering expensive watches to think of doing such a dirty chore.

I halfheartedly sprinkled some of the green powder onto the greasy film in the sink, rubbed it around a little with the rag, ran clean water to rinse it out, and gingerly dropped the gritty, soggy rag onto the crumpled paper towels in the wastebasket underneath the sink. Then I sat down on a high stool at the rear of the shop to nibble on peanuts and read the supply of comic books I had brought to the store to keep me occupied while I was waiting to run the next delivery.

I hadn't turned the first page before I heard my uncle bellowing out at me.

"Sidney! Come back here! You call this sink clean?"

"It looks clean to me," I lied, looking at how smudgy and gritty I had left it.

"Well, you need to have your eyes examined, then," he said, handing me the can of scouring powder again. "Now get your rag and clean it right, this time."

It nearly killed me to fish that nasty rag out of the wastebasket and scour the sink again. I don't think I did a much better job the second time, but I knew it would be the last time I'd ever have to clean *that* sink. It was almost five o'clock, and when five o'clock came, I would head for home and never go back to that job. I never did, either. The nerve of Uncle Abe, expecting *me* to clean a sink!

In my first two jobs, I had set a pattern that would last me for a good long time, letting someone else take over for me when the going was rough, not stooping to do what was required of me, taking only the best parts, the fun parts, the acclaim, for myself and leaving the drudgery, the cleanup, for someone else.

Chapter Five

Dead Center

I began really moving up in the world in my own estimation when I started palling around with Johnny Spitzberg. Johnny was a couple of years older than I was, but I had known him all my life, because his mother and mine were best friends. Johnny was everything I wasn't. He was a fantastic dancer, a skilled athlete, and he had a reputation for being good with women. Johnny belonged to the Wilner branch of AZA, a Jewish fraternity in our high school, and he told me he could get me in, too. I wanted to join, because I thought that would automatically mean I'd have some friends, I'd be popular, and naturally, I'd be invited to all the AZA parties.

At the first meeting to which I was invited, I had to stand in the middle of a circle of members while they asked me a lot of questions. I tried to give dignified, man-of-the-world answers, especially to the question about why I wanted to join Wilner. I rattled off some high-sounding stuff about how such high caliber kids belonged, that I wanted to associate with them, and that I hoped to contribute something to the organization. It was a snow job, but they seemed pleased at my answers. I noticed a couple of them polishing their fingernails on their shoulders, being cocky and pleased with themselves. Their smiles made me think they were pleased with me, too, and as my confidence grew, my defenses let down, so I was not prepared for the next question. When they asked, "What do you think of girls?" I didn't prepare a suave, smooth, sharp answer for them. I just said, with sophomoric naivete, "Aw, they're all right."

The whole room burst into uproarious laughter, and I blushed a billion shades of red and purple. It really seemed to break them up, but I was accepted into the club anyway.

Thinking about how they had laughed at my answer, I wondered if maybe, just maybe, I would go into show business as a comedian like my uncle, Jay Jason, who had worked the nightclub circuit.

I had a chance to try out my acting ability when I went to my first AZA convention in Richmond. There we played poker, told dirty jokes, and some of the kids got drunk. I was a little high myself, relaxed enough not to be self-conscious, and I really put on an act, pretending that I was dead drunk, staggering down the stairs, muttering hilariously stupid remarks, and falling all over myself. My new friends talked for a long time afterward about how perfectly crazy I was when I was drunk in Richmond, and I knew I was on my way.

AZA continued to provide a kind of security and sense of accomplishment for me during the rest of high school. I wrote a humorous skit that was a big success, and eventually I became an officer in the chapter. The first tastes of success instead of failure in my life made me resolve that I would make up for my poor showing in high school by really making it in college.

During the summer between my graduation from high school and my first year at American University, I stayed with my grandmother in Atlantic City and worked on the boardwalk as a pitchman for a handwriting analysis booth. There I learned that I was good at persuading people to shell out their money. My budding confidence made me act so grown-up, so sure of myself, that

I was actually approached by a prostitute one night. I walked away from her, my knees shaking, but I didn't fail to tell my friends all the details, embroidered with my fertile imagination.

It was clear to me from the bug-eyed way they listened, that I was really coming up in their estimation. One of them told me privately later, "You know, Sid, you used to be about the biggest klutz in town. But you've changed somehow. Now you act more like just one of the guys." He was so impressed, I knew he would be spreading the word around. Since I had arrived in his eyes, I had arrived in my own eyes, too.

All of a sudden, food began to take a back seat in my life. After all, there were more interesting things to do than just stuff myself all the time. There were parties, and girls, and all sorts of extracurricular activities. It was a brand-new world, but I was still in the dead-center of it.

As I sat waiting for my first job interview in the placement office of American University, I looked over some of the letters of recommendation in my dossier.

The first one, from the Dean of Students, read,

> *Mr. Roth is a serious, pleasant, and sincere young man. He has a friendly disposition and a courteous reserved manner. He is well above the average in scholastic ability and intelligence. He is stable and reliable . . . has high standards of ethics and adheres to strong moral principles. He is recommended highly for any position for which he is professionally or technically qualified.*

The next letter, from one of my professors, said,

> *Sidney has been a student in my classes in which he did excellent work. I have also had occasion to work with him in student organizations in which he was always to be counted*

on to do a fine job in every way. He has ambition, takes pride in his work, and will be successful at whatever he attempts. I recommend him highly.

Another said,

He has taken a leadership position on campus and is well-respected by his fellow students as well as by his teachers.

As I read over these references, pride oozed from my every pore. I patted myself on the back that I had come a long way from the mamma's baby high school fatso who couldn't even make a decent grade without cheating, who couldn't fend for himself in any conflict. Now, here I was, slim, popular, about to be a university graduate with a major in public relations. The world lay waiting at my feet.

I had chosen public relations for my major when I was a freshman, hardly knowing what the subject meant, just because someone told me it was an easy major. Nevertheless, it had proved to be the right one for me. My own public relations had soared, my name had been on the Dean's honor roll, I had been president of a large Campus organization, my social life was top-drawer, and my parents had bought me a new Chevy convertible as a reward for my good grades. On top of everything else, I had won the coveted Glover Leadership Scholarship in my senior year.

I stood at least ten feet tall when the receptionist called my name and I strode into the office for my job interview with a man from the New York Port Authority. I was wearing a brand-new suit, shoes shined to perfection and a Florida tan acquired during the recent semester break, and I was carrying those terrific references under my arm. The job was a difficult one to obtain, I had been told, but I was positive it was mine if I wanted it.

Later, the vocational counselor broke the news to me.

"You didn't get the job, Sid. Tough, man. The Port Authority representative said you acted like you thought the world owed you a living. He said you'd probably have two or three jobs before you'd realize the world doesn't revolve around you."

It stung, but I was aware that the vocational counselor was looking at me closely, to see how I would take it, so I just gave a disgusted snort at their stupidity and walked out.

What the Port Authority man had said would prove to be the understatement of the century. However, it didn't take long for me to discount it entirely, deciding he had some kind of a hang-up. He was probably jealous that I was so young and "with it," while he was on his way down and out the back door. He'd probably give the job to some old dodo, I rationalized, just so *he* could keep on feeling superior, polishing up his sick ego. That I was utterly consumed with polishing mine was hidden from my eyes. I was "Mister It."

After I had fully rationalized my way out of my failure to get the job with the Port Authority, my self-confidence swelled up bigger than ever, and I landed a job doing PR work for a department-store chain in Rochester, New York. I said good-bye to my family and was off to make my million and conquer the world.

For a few weeks, I did well at my job. But then a supervisor came down to Rochester, just to see how things were going. We were in the midst of a rush promotion, and everyone in the office had been asked to help assemble and staple materials for distribution.

The biggest wheels in the office were manning staplers without complaint, even my boss and my boss's boss, just to get the job done. But I wasn't interested in sticking with something that dull, and after assembling a few packets, I went back to my desk and found something more interesting to occupy my valuable time.

The next week, my supervisor called me into his office. There were no preliminaries.

"Sid, remember when everybody except you was stapling promotional packets last week?"

"Yes," I acknowledged, wondering what was coming next.

"Well," he went on, "I hate to do this, but you really asked for it. I've been instructed to terminate you."

Unlike me, my supervisor was a man who believed in following his instructions.

My indignation flared. It was the case of the workroom sink all over again. He learned that I considered stapling *anything* to be a menial chore, far beneath my ability. After all, I was Sid Roth, one of the top grads of American University, with all those great credentials! And they expected me to staple things together? Any crummy kid with no education at all could do that!

Before I could quit, I was fired. The Rochester department store had no place for a man with my attitude. My first career job had lasted almost two months.

What was it the Port Authority man had said? That I would have two or three jobs before I realized the world didn't revolve around me? Ha! I'd show them.

When I returned home, I pretended that I had resigned my job in order to further my education by attending law school at George Washington University.

I didn't really want to go to law school, but I had to save face somehow. And this seemed as good a way as any. Besides, from what I had observed, lawyers were always right in the midst of everything having to do with money. Maybe my first million would come as Sid Roth, Attorney-at-Law.

My father was delighted. He took me to one of the finest stores in the city and bought me four new suits—conservative solid colors and pin stripes with vests—exactly what the most well-heeled young lawyer would wear. I looked the picture of success. My father went around bragging to everyone about how well I had done in the University, and how I was now on my way to becoming a rich and successful attorney.

But there was a flag on the play.

In college, I had found that there was nothing I couldn't learn if I worked hard. But in law school, although I was keeping up with my assignments, some of the professors were beginning to lose me. I could see the handwriting on the wall. Not wanting to flunk out, I just quit going to class. I didn't bother to notify the school of my intentions, although I realized that early notification was necessary if I wanted a refund. After all, why should I worry? It wasn't my money, it belonged to my parents. They had paid for everything.

After Mom realized I'd quit school, she telephoned the business office and asked them to give her a tuition refund, but it was too late. The refund deadline had passed. I took all my expensive, brand-new law books and sold them at a secondhand bookstore for next to nothing, thinking that they had been an awful waste of money. A pity. I was only glad it was my parents' money and not mine.

Chapter Six

Big Deal

I wanted to get into something more exciting than school, some thing with glamour in it. The most exciting career I could think of was show business. I had spent several summers during college vacation chauffeuring my comedian uncle, Jay Jason, from one engagement to another at resorts in the Catskill Mountains. Show business had gotten into my blood then. I had also done a little songwriting and produced a couple of records during my college years. And there was my acclaimed drunk imitation in high school. Maybe show business was where I belonged.

I went to New Jersey to see my uncle and asked him if he could help me get started.

"Yeah, sure, Sid," he said, eager to help me get going. "You don't have any talent of your own, to speak of, but you're a born promoter. And you have your public relations degree. Why don't you go into the talent-scout business? I know a guy who could use an extra leg man. There wouldn't be any money in it at first, but he could show you the ropes."

He introduced me to Miles Millard, and I was off and running, sunglasses and all, looking more like Hollywood than the people who lived there.

For the first two months, I didn't do much except type contracts, listen to the negotiations between performers and Miles Millard, and ride the subways delivering official-looking papers here and there. It wasn't really too different from my old job of delivering watches for my Uncle Abe, but it looked big-time. I was staying with my uncle, so I didn't need much money, and I was promised a percentage of the contract for any new talent I brought into the agency.

I went everywhere looking for unrecognized talent, dreaming that I would "discover" an Elvis Presley and make, not one million, but several million, in short order. I could taste success. But where was the talent? I couldn't find any worth promoting.

And then, one rainy Friday afternoon, it happened. Nothing much had been going on, and we were about to lock up and call it a day when the impossible dream walked in. He was an obviously talented, terrifically good-looking young singer whose star was on the rise, and he was actually *looking* for an agency to represent him. His contract was owned by some relatives of his who were gangsters. They paid his expenses, gave him a salary, and collected the rest of the take for themselves. That worked pretty well while he was an unknown, but now he was moving up so fast, they needed a legitimate front for him, an on-the-level recognized agency to represent him while they stayed in the background. He'd get to the top quicker, that way. We all agreed that the top was where he was destined to go.

The gangsters didn't want to come to our office to work out the details of how we would represent the boy, but they invited me to come to dinner at their place the next evening so we could come to a firm agreement and sign contracts all around.

Miles and I sat up half the night getting the papers ready. It was cloak and dagger all the way. I wasn't told where to come. A couple members of the gang picked me and Jim Brody up. Jim was a public relations man, too, a friend of mine who just happened to be in the office that afternoon. They invited him to come along. We drove through dark alleys I'd never seen before, and stopped in front of a dingy dry-cleaning shop on a rubbish-littered side street. The shop was closed, but one of the men had a key that let us in. Bells on the door set up a crazy clanging as it swung open, and I nearly jumped out of my skin. I didn't feel nearly as cool, confident, and a master of the situation as I thought my clothes and oversized dark glasses made me look.

After we had brushed our way past rows and rows of rack-hung clothes, almost overpowering me with the smell of dry-cleaning fluid, we emerged into a bright and crowded kitchen where half a dozen guys were yelling at one another, stirring spaghetti in a huge pot, and gesticulating wildly.

I nodded curtly at everyone, kept my dark glasses on, my eyes and ears open, and my mouth shut. I could see there was no point in trying to talk business until things had calmed down a little.

When the spaghetti was cooked, someone shoved a chair at me, and we all sat down at the big kitchen table with red plaid oilcloth on it. Books, papers, vases of flowers, cigar boxes, a sewing kit, and other paraphernalia of family living were shoved out of the way to make room for great platters full of steaming spaghetti piled high with succulent meatballs and tomato sauce, the most delicious I had ever eaten. There were even elegantly huge white linen napkins to be tucked around our necks.

Bending over the spaghetti and the hot bread that was crusty on the outside, steaming soft on the inside, I momentarily forgot the reason for my visit. Eventually, however, all the plates were empty, and chairs were tipped back from the table. Cigars were passed, more coffee was poured, and I was introduced to everybody as a representative of the talent office that was going to handle their singer.

Very businesslike, I opened my attache case and began to pull out the various forms I needed to present to them for discussion and their signatures to make the deal official. Before I had finished extracting the papers, however, Jim Brody opened his mouth and began to talk. My mouth fell open, too, in astonishment at what I heard coming out of his.

"You know," he said, in a confidential tone that indicated he was doing them a very great favor, "you guys shouldn't let that Miles Millard Agency represent the kid. Why, that Millard is incredibly cheap. He has more talent leaving him than he has coming in. Everybody's getting disgusted about what a lousy promoter he is. Nobody gets to the top once they sign with him."

Jim paused, scowled thoughtfully at his cigar for a breathless moment, and then delivered the final pronouncement: "A Millard contract is the quickest way to the bottom of the ladder, and any fool ought to be able to get to the bottom easy enough all by himself without paying Millard a percentage to help him tumble down." He finally stopped talking to laugh long and hard about what a cheapskate my boss was. After a few seconds of looking quizzically at one another, the tension broke, and everyone began to guffaw right along with him. One of them doubled over in merriment, so relieved that they hadn't made the mistake of signing with the outfit I represented.

I just sat there, trembling, the papers in my hands. I was too dumbfounded to know what to say. Trouble was, I knew Brody was right. We *didn't* have any good talent left in our agency. The truth was, we probably *would* run their singer straight into the ground, too.

When they had laughed themselves out, the gangsters all turned toward Brody with their questions.

"Yeah? Tell us more about all that? Can you prove it? Like for instance, who's leaving the agency now? And what outfit do you think we should sign up with?"

Jim had all the right answers for them; they believed him. Nobody asked me a thing. I was ignored just as completely as if I hadn't even been there.

I was glad no one was looking. It was impossible to keep the pain from showing on my face. I knew that everything Jim was saying was true; it had been true from the beginning, from the time I first went to work with Miles to learn the business. But I had kept telling myself that once we found a really great piece of talent, things would be different. And now I saw all my dreams—of traveling with the kid, staying at swanky Miami hotels, wining and dining with the biggest names in show business—disappearing down the drain. My grandiose plans for spending my millions were all kaput. Worse than that, no one even offered to take me home. I let myself out on the side street and walked for blocks to the subway, then took the long, late, bus ride to Teaneck, New Jersey, where my uncle lived. When I finally reached his house, I peeled off my beautiful suit and fell into bed, bone-weary and utterly discouraged, at the bottom of the world.

The next day, my former PR friend came by the office and clapped his hand on my shoulder before I could move out of his reach.

"Sid," he said, "you know, you're really a basically nice guy. You don't belong in this business. You don't know how rough these syndicate people can play. By fouling up the deal for you last night, I really did you a big favor—because I like you."

Friendship like that I could do without. I didn't have to say a word. He read it in my face. And I never saw him again. Miles Millard didn't seem too upset. "Win a few, lose a few," he said when I told him how Brody had stolen the show at the dinner party. But he didn't urge me to stay on with his firm when I told him I thought it was time for me to head back to D.C. I had wasted three months, not even being able to support myself, let alone earning a million dollars. There was no future for me or anybody else in working with Miles Millard's talent agency. There must be the right job for me somewhere else, just waiting for me to come along.

Chapter Seven

Mr. Cool

I went back home to live with my parents again. That was hard after tasting independence from their interference while I was living in New Jersey. But I settled in and went to work for my watch repairman Uncle Abe again, this time as sales manager for his more than 100 retail pick-up locations. It was a stop-gap job. I was just marking time while I was waiting for the great one to turn up. But this time, my uncle had someone else acting as his errand boy, so he didn't ask me to scrub any sinks.

I kept in touch with a local employment agency, and I stopped by often to read through the lists of new job openings. I got acquainted with the agency manager as the weeks rolled by, and one day after I'd been working for my uncle about four months, the employment agency itself had an opening for a job counselor. The pay would be better than what I was getting with my uncle, the future couldn't be any more nonexistent, and working in the agency, I'd have first crack at any good jobs that came along.

About this time, I moved out of my folks' house and into an apartment with Art Creedsman, one of my college buddies. My folks had been about to bug me to death. No matter what time of night I got in, Mom would always call out and ask me where I'd been, with whom, what I'd been doing, whether I'd had a good time or not, and all that. I had to get out from under. After I moved to the apartment, Mom still called me on the telephone a lot, but that wasn't quite so bad. If I didn't feel like talking, I could always tell her there was someone at the door and promise to call her back later.

One night there really *was* someone at the door. Art and I were sitting in the living room, drinking beer and just talking, when somebody pounded on the door, real heavy, like he wasn't going to stop until we let him in. Art and I looked at each other, wondering who it was, then he went to the door. I got up too, to be the back-up man in case he needed one. When Art opened the door just a crack, it shot out of his hand and banged against the wall.

Chuck Hoffman literally threw himself into the room, and practically collapsed on the couch. I had known Chuck in college, and he'd always seemed a little bit nervous to me. Now he was huffing and puffing, completely out of breath, and he looked scared to death. Art got him a beer, and when he had simmered down a little, he started talking.

"It's the worst thing that's ever happened to me in my whole entire life!" he gasped. "I don't know what I'm going to do with her."

He seemed so upset that I thought something awful must have happened. I had visions of his having killed someone and stuffed her into the trunk of his car. Maybe he was worried about how he was going to dispose of the body, and whether or not the police would catch him. But it turned out that nothing quite that drastic was involved.

Chuck had been staying in a roominghouse. He had given his landlady a rather large deposit in advance. Too late, he had discovered that his landlady was an alcoholic, and her "house" was too rowdy for his taste. One night Chuck overheard her having a violent argument with her husband, an argument in which they were threatening to kill each other. Chuck was so paranoid, he thought they meant to kill him before they killed each other, and he was scared to go back to his room even to get his things, much less to ask for the return of his deposit.

I saw at once how to get his money back for him, and have someone to help Art and me with our apartment expenses at the same time. It was just the kind of action I relished, me with my persuasive manner.

"Relax, Chuck," I told him, winking at Art. "You can sleep on the couch here tonight, and tomorrow we'll help you get your green stuff back."

Art looked at me and shrugged, as if he didn't know what to do with either one of us. Chuck unlaced his shoes and stretched out on the couch.

The next morning, I put on my sunglasses and went with Chuck to the roominghouse, taking a little Brownie camera and a notebook along in my briefcase. When the landlady came to answer the door, I nodded toward Chuck and said, "I've come with Mr. Hoffman here to get his things and to get his deposit back. I understand he left quite a substantial amount of money with you?"

She hiccupped, put her hand to her mouth in apology, and started to close the door.

"Oh, we can't (hiccup) give deposits back," she said. "They're to (hiccup) cover the cost of (burp) . . ."

I had my foot in the doorway by then, and when the door came against it, I shoved it open and stepped authoritatively into the foyer, put my briefcase on a small table, and took out my camera.

While Chuck bounded up the stairs, taking them two at a time, to get his things, I lifted the camera to my eye. Aiming through the archway into a sitting room, I snapped the shutter, and advanced the imaginary film to position for the next shot. Then I aimed the camera right at the landlady.

She just stood there, her mouth hanging open, and finally sputtered, "What the—? Just (hiccup) what do you think (hiccup) you're doing?"

"Taking pictures for evidence for the lawsuit, ma'am," I said, matter of factly. After clicking off a few more frames, I put the camera back in the briefcase and picked up my notebook. Chuck was back downstairs, suits hanging over his arm, his suitcase bulging.

"Now, Mrs. Landon," I said, "I wonder if you'd mind answering a few questions for me. We understand you had a big argument with your husband, and—"

Before I could finish the first question, she had rushed into a back bedroom, come out with her pocketbook, and was peeling bills off and handing them to Chuck faster than I could count them.

I had a hard time maintaining my dignity until we were back outside and a block away in my car. Then I had to pull over to the curb just to explode in laughter.

"The way you pulled that off," Chuck said, real admiration in his eyes, "you've missed your calling, Sid. You should have been a con man."

I thought maybe he was right, but I didn't know quite how to get into that business. One thing was for sure: I was getting tired of the employment agency. All those forms to fill out. What a drag. There must be something better. It didn't occur to me then that Chuck was going to be my partner in finding it.

One night, Chuck and I were by ourselves in the apartment. I was sitting in the only really comfortable chair, reading the want ads, Chuck was sprawled on the floor, fiddling with a little transistor radio.

"Nothing but folk music," he muttered. "Guitars and folk music. Wouldn't you think there'd be a little more variety on the airwaves?" He sounded thoroughly disgusted, snapped the radio off, and sat up to lean against the record player. We started talking about fads in entertainment and decided that folk music must have reached an all-time high in popularity.

"You know," he said, "I'll bet there's a lot of high school talent in folk music these days."

"Yeah," I agreed. "Most any high school must have a dozen kids who can twang the guitar and sing some of that stuff."

The idea occurred to both of us at once, and we were off and running with it. Why not? A talent contest in every high school, the winners to be taped for radio presentation, listeners to write in their votes for their favorite.

In less than fifteen minutes, we had worked out the whole format for a show to be called "Hootenanny." The talent would work for little or nothing to be given a showcase. Chuck and I could share the work of setting the contests up, we could pocket the profits of outside concerts and clean up on donations contributed by the sponsors.

It was a natural, for both of us. Chuck's job was to line up the high schools, schedule the programs, and handle all the boring behind-the-scenes details. I would be the front man, the guy at the microphone who introduced the contestants, who auditioned the talent. Chuck did as much work as I did, maybe more, and we received equal billing on programs and advertisements as producers of "Hootenanny." But I was the one everyone saw.

The first radio station we approached with our idea was enthusiastic. They gave us a six-week contract, and hired us as producers at seventy-five dollars a week for each of us. Since that wasn't enough to live on, I hung on to my employment agency job for the time being.

For our first concert, we packed the gym at American University, and the radio station was ecstatic over the response to the program. The audience grew week by week, and when the first six weeks were almost over, the station was eager to renew the contract with Chuck and me as producers.

We wanted to continue with the program, all right, but I got to thinking that there wasn't really enough money in it for both of us. Instead of doing the decent thing, talking it over with Chuck, and offering to buy out his interest, I decided to make him quit.

Cutting out my co-producer wasn't hard. I began by deliberately disagreeing with him whenever an occasion arose. I started arguments over nothing. I would belittle him in front of other people, criticizing him for how he handled his share of the work, generally making life as miserable as I could for him. When he showed signs of weakening, I embarked on a little more intensive psychological warfare. Knowing he was easy to rattle, a nervous type to begin with, I hit upon the idea of tapping on the wall of his bedroom every night when he was trying to go to sleep. I got a kind of diabolical pleasure out of seeing him stagger out in the morning, frustrated from lack of sleep. He knew I was doing the tapping, but I would always act innocent, and try to make him think he was just hearing things, that he was probably going off his rocker.

"Chuck, for your own good, you ought to see a shrink," I told him.

One night when Art was out, Chuck came storming out of his room and into mine, all but frothing at the mouth, he was so angry with me.

"Okay, Mr. Producer!" he yelled. "You can have the show, you can have the apartment, you can have your infernal wall tapping! You can have whatever you want! I've had it!"

I don't know where he slept that night, but the next day, he came back, packed his things, and disappeared from my life. That left me as sole producer of my own show, getting all the glory *and* all the money for myself.

I quit my job with the employment agency and spent all my time in show biz, conducting talent contests, acting as an agent for our performers, scheduling nightclub acts, and taking as hefty a cut from all the proceeds as I could get by with. The dark glasses were full-time props for me now. I was Mr. Cool himself. The first million would soon be in sight.

Chapter Eight

Blurred Signposts

"Sid, they always have the prettiest girls at these Young Democrats meetings," my buddy, Joe Garfinkle, was saying.

"You ought to know," I grinned at him. "And I'm willing to find out."

Joe was ten years older than I was, but I liked to go places with him because he always knew where the best parties were—and the best-looking women. I wasn't interested in *all* the girls, just some of them. They had to be good-looking, but they didn't have to be "good."

As we sauntered into the meeting room that night, I saw a girl across the room with the most beautiful smile I had ever seen.

"Hey, Joe!—Get a load of *that* one!" I made a silent whistle, waiting for him to introduce me.

"You're on your own, kid," he chuckled. "I've never seen that particular doll before. Can't help you none. Now that one over there—" he gestured somewhere off to our right—"she's more my style. I *do* know her already, from *way* back. And how! Umm humh!"

He headed over in that direction, and I made a beeline for the blonde with the smile that lit up the room. I gave her my standard line.

"Say, I'm planning a great party at my apartment in a week or two," I said. How about writing your name and phone number on this piece of paper so maybe I can let you know—"

She turned off the smile and looked at me as if she wasn't sure at first whether she ought to give me the information or not, but then she took my pencil and wrote something on the paper. I stuffed it in my pocket, and we talked about nothing for a few minutes. She told me she should be studying for a Spanish test she was going to have the next day. That didn't sound too exciting, so I left her standing alone in order to collect a few more names and phone numbers. Never could tell when a few extra girls would come in handy for a party—or something.

Later in the evening, I noticed that Joe was talking to the girl. That bothered me, somehow. I had never felt exactly that way before, and wondered why I was feeling it now. Something like jealousy maybe? After all, there was no reason why Joe shouldn't talk to her. She wasn't my girl, or anything like that. I didn't even know her, hadn't even read the slip of paper she had put her name on. I dug it out of my pocket and read the name. Joy, it said. Joy Young. It was a nice-sounding name.

A couple of weeks later, I telephoned Joy and asked her for a date. When I picked her up, I learned that she had a Corvette of her own. In my mind, any girl who had her own Corvette was bound to be rich.

When I was in college, I had made up my mind to marry a wealthy girl. After all, there was no point in investing my life in someone who didn't have something material of her own to contribute.

I was further impressed by the fact that when we went out to eat, Joy ordered the cheapest entree instead of the most expensive. And I was amazed at how easy she was to get along with. When I suggested that we might go to a movie, she agreed with me right away on which one we ought to see.

Before I had dated Joy half a dozen times, I was counting off her good qualities: she was clean-cut, agreeable, had class, was even-tempered, considerate, rich, and so pretty that I could feel myself falling in love with her. She had all the qualifications I looked for in a girl, except that she seemed to be a "nice" girl. That usually made a girl uninteresting to me, but even that was a decided plus in someone I might want to spend the rest of my life with.

There was only one hitch. Joy was a Gentile. But most of the Jewish girls I had dated had been too bossy to suit me, hard to get along with. Well, Joy would just have to convert to Judaism, that was all. Then everything about her would be super-kosher.

Joy had gotten serious about me, too. I realized it one night when she paused outside her apartment door and said that maybe we shouldn't see one another anymore.

"How come?" I asked her, so sure of what I wanted I couldn't see any reason to break off.

"Well, we're getting too serious to be just friends, and we do have these different religions after all."

The more she talked about the difficulties, the better I realized that she was the one for me. I didn't argue, I just took her in my arms and shushed her with kisses. The next day, I gave my class ring to Uncle Abe so he could make it into a charm for her bracelet. When she accepted it with that radiant smile of hers, that made it official in my mind. Joy was my girl, and someday she would be my wife.

"Mom, you know this Joy I've told you about, the Gentile girl I've been dating? I want to bring her to Shirley's wedding, and let her meet you and Dad and some of the rest of the family."

I wasn't really too eager to put Joy in the midst of the mob of relatives, but she'd have to meet them sometime, and at my sister's wedding they would all be together.

"Sid, you're kidding me! You want to bring a shiksa to Shirley's wedding? She'll just feel out of place." Mom was about to dismiss my request lightly, but then she looked at me more closely, and suspicion dawned in her eyes.

"Sidney, you're not thinking—You *can't* be thinking of *marrying* a girl who's not Jewish?" Mom put one hand over her heart, sank down panting into an overstuffed chair, and began to fan herself with a newspaper. There flashed through my mind the one time in my childhood when Mom didn't let me have my own way. She hadn't scolded me or punished me, she had just started screaming, like I did when I was having a tantrum. She had kept it up until I backed down. Surely she wasn't going to give me a hard time about Joy. I'd have to pull out all the stops to keep her from doing that.

"Mom, you want me to be happy, don't you?" I pleaded, making my voice sound like a little boy again. "I'm in love with Joy. There's no other girl for me, and besides, she can hardly wait to convert to Judaism so she can fit in with the rest of the family."

That was a bald-faced lie. The only time we had seriously talked about our different religious backgrounds, Joy had suggested that I become a Baptist instead. That was out of the question, but I knew I could talk her into doing what I wanted her to do. There was no way my father would ever accept her otherwise. Besides, Joy's upbringing as a Baptist hadn't seemed that important to her. She hadn't once gone to church in all the time I'd known her.

"*She wants to convert?*" Mom was still eyeing me suspiciously, but the tempo of her fanning had slowed to a mere occasional flapping of the newspaper.

"Yeah," I said again. "We'll be going to see the rabbi to get her started on her instructions as soon as you break the news to Dad and make the arrangements for us."

"Well, I don't know what your father will think about her coming to the wedding." I could see that Mom's agile mind was in gear, figuring the best tactics to use to persuade Dad, and then I laid down my high card.

"Mom, you'll just have to tell him that if Joy can't come with me, I won't be at the wedding either." From the stricken look that flashed across her face, I knew I had it made.

"It's ridiculous that anyone would think that Joy shouldn't come to the wedding," Mom snorted, in full sail for the attack against my father. "After all, she's going to be our daughter-in-law, and your father ought to be proud you'll be marrying someone who will convert and bring your children up right."

My cause was as good as accomplished. My secret weapon had never failed me yet.

Shirley's wedding was a real extravaganza, far more elegant even than my bar mitzvah. There was an elaborate sit-down dinner for all the wedding guests, an eight-piece orchestra for the dancing afterward, gorgeous ice sculptures, flowers everywhere you looked, and food, food, food.

When I introduced Joy to my parents, my father scowled at her, said hello in the sternest voice he owned, and shook hands woodenly. Then Mother concentrated on keeping Dad on one side of the room while I kept Joy on the other.

All the other relatives crowded around to meet Joy, to look her over. They knew she must be something special to me or I wouldn't have brought her to the wedding. Although they were too polite to ask out loud, I could see the questions in everyone's eyes:

"What's with this Joy who's with Sidney?"

"Is he going to marry her?"

"She looks like a shiksa."

"What's her old man's business?"

But I wasn't ready to answer anybody's questions, spoken or unspoken. I didn't know my own timetable yet. I had just received a draft notice from Uncle Sam, and was to report for an induction examination the next week. I thought I'd be given a 4-F classification because of my bad hip, but I couldn't be sure. My classification would have some bearing on my plans for the immediate future. I would just have to wait and see, and so would all my relatives. I'd tell them my intentions when it was time for them to buy our wedding presents. That would be soon enough.

When I got on the bus with the rest of the fellows scheduled for induction examinations at Fort Hollabird, Maryland, I sat down next to a fellow I'd known since grade school. He told me that he had been married and divorced and that now he was "gay." Living with his male companion in New York City, where they were fashion designers, he was happy with his arrangement. To *each his own*, I thought. It was his business what he wanted to do with his life, just as it was my business what I did with mine.

At Fort Hollabird, all of us had to strip to the skin and walk single file through several lines in which doctors tapped and listened, probed and peered. Then we got dressed and went to the last inspection station. I handed x-rays of my hip to the attendants there, and was rewarded with an automatic 4-F classification. When my buddy handed over his psychiatrist's report, he was given an exempt-from-service classification, too.

As soon as I could, I got to a telephone to give Joy the news. I could tell from the tone of her voice that she was about to cry with relief.

"Oh, Sidney," she said, "I'm so happy! I could just see you being sent far away, to Germany, or someplace like that. And maybe I'd never see you again."

It shook me up that she cared that much.

The next morning, when I was combing my hair, I noticed that it was getting awfully thin on top. "I bet I'll really look ugly when I'm bald," I complained out loud to myself. Both of my grandfathers were bald; it ran in the family. Maybe I should get married while I was still handsome enough for Joy to be interested in me.

I was surprised when my rabbi tried to talk me out of marrying Joy. I thought he'd be happy that she had agreed to convert.

"Are you sure that Joy is the only girl in the whole world who can make you happy, Sidney?" he asked me, tamping tobacco down in his corncob pipe. Sitting there in his book-lined study, I could see that he didn't want a superficial answer. He wanted me to really probe my soul about the whole matter of marrying a Gentile. Feeling I had done my part by talking Joy into converting, I didn't think I should have to tackle the rabbi, so I suddenly remembered a previous nonexistent engagement and went home to sic my invincible secret weapon on him.

Mom dived in with no holds barred, certain that she would lose her son if his wife-to-be was not permitted to become a Jew. No man in his right mind dared stand up to my mother, rabbi or not. The next thing I knew, the rabbi was on the telephone, wanting to speak to me. He sounded eager to start Joy's instruction in Judaism.

Under the hammering of my mom's daily influence, even my dad was becoming almost persuaded that a converted Jewish daughter-in-law was actually preferable to one who had merely been born into the faith.

We decided on a small wedding at my parents' home. Since Joy had converted to Judaism, her parents weren't interested in throwing a big wedding, and a lavish Jewish wedding didn't seem appropriate either.

On March 15, 1964, Joy and I said our vows before the rabbi under a huppah in my parents' living room. There were only a few relatives present as Joy and I drank from the fragile wine glass and then I smashed it with my foot, symbolizing the destruction of the Temple in Jerusalem. That was supposed to remind us that our marriage might be broken, too, unless it was under God's protection.

But if I knew nothing about the significance of the destruction of the Temple, I knew less about the need for God's protection in a marriage. The only thing I thought about as I heard the crunch of the glass under my foot was that now I had a beautiful wife, to do for me all the things a wife was expected to do.

"My people are destroyed from lack of knowledge," God's Word said (Hosea 4:6). But I was traveling so fast down the road leading to destruction that the signposts blurred beyond reading as I sped by them.

Chapter Nine

Something More?

A few weeks before our wedding, I talked to the manager of the radio station over which "Hootenanny" was aired.

"Say," I told him, "I'm going to get married soon. How about using your influence with one of our sponsors—to see if he'd give me the honeymoon suite in the Summit Hotel for a few days?"

"Congratulations, Sid," he said, shifting his cigar to the corner of his mouth, and giving me a hearty handshake. "I expect it's all booked up. But best regards, anyway."

"Best regards, anyway." That's what I got from several people who called to cancel bookings for folk music programs. A longhaired singing group from England called "The Beatles" had come onto the scene. Folk music was passe overnight, and a week before the wedding, my show went off the air.

New wife, new apartment, new furniture, and no job. Joy's knight in shining armor, the big wheel, strong, successful, and glamourous, turned into an unshaven reader of want ads, lazing around the apartment in wrinkled Bermuda shorts, waiting for his working wife to come home and cook dinner for him. Without the prestige of my position to keep my ego boosted, I reverted to being a complaining, surly, selfish, demanding mamma's boy. I began to see something other than hero worship in Joy's eyes when she came in tired from work at five-thirty every day and found that I, who had been loafing around all day watching TV, expected her to wait on me.

For a couple of months, I made a halfhearted attempt to sell real estate on a commission basis, but I wasn't successful at it, and brought in very little income. Then one day when I was sitting around, I picked up a *Reader's Digest* and read an article written by a health officer in the venereal disease (VD) branch of the Department of Health, Education and Welfare (HEW). The account of his adventures in going to houses of ill repute, talking to prostitutes, and interviewing nightclub habitues about their sexual contacts sounded most intriguing to me. Why, he was like an FBI agent almost.

I called the local office of HEW to see if there were any job openings available in that type of work, told them something of my education and job experience, and was scheduled to be interviewed for an opening in Miami, Florida. I learned later that the interviewer thought I had a greater potential for success in the job than anyone else who had ever applied with them. The job was mine.

Joy was excited at the prospect of moving to Florida. It seemed that it would be like a perpetual vacation, and she hated her secretarial job in Washington. We packed up to move, and I enrolled in the training course to be a health officer in the VD department of HEW.

The training course emphasized the symptoms and history of VD, the best interviewing techniques, and how to get an individual to open up and tell you who his sex partners had been. I learned not to be shocked or surprised at anything.

After a few weeks training, I put on my dark glasses again and was back in the glamour (I thought) of the working world. But the men conducting the training course had neglected to mention my bugaboo. I was required to draw blood from suspects.

My first experience at performing that operation nearly threw me. I kept thinking there would be someone else who would handle that aspect of it, but I was mistaken. I had to roll the man's sleeve up; I had to knot the rubber hose around his arm; I had to ask him to make a fist while I punched around, looking for a large-enough vein; I had to jab and jab again trying to get the needle in the right place; I had to pull the plunger back and back until the vial was filled with the dark red venous blood. Then I had to remember to tell him to relax his fist before I withdrew the needle, so that the blood wouldn't spurt out all over me. Every single step of the operation was calculated to make me sick at my stomach.

On top of all that, some of the places I was required to go were about as far from glamourous as anyone could possibly imagine. My interviewees were never scantily clad, perfumed beauties backstage in glittering nightclubs. I remember one day, sweltering in the heat, perching on the edge of a broken-down, absolutely filthy couch, breathing dirt and dust, trying to get a blood sample from a toothless hag who had on a rag of a housedress with nothing under it. The stench was overpowering, her list of contacts seemingly endless. I could hear mice scurrying through the walls, and dead cockroaches were lying all over the floor.

If I hadn't been flat broke, with no savings to fall back on, no way to get to Washington, no other way to pay rent or buy groceries, I'd have quit after the first unglamourous, bloody day. But I had no choice but to stay with it.

Eventually, the endless repetition dulled the horror of it for me, and I took so many blood samples that it became routine. But I always hated the job.

The job didn't like me, either. My boss was a perfectionist, and it didn't seem to cut any ice at all with him that I was such an excellent interviewer, such a bright young man with so many ideas for improving operations and cutting down on paperwork in the office. At my first suggestion, he let it be known that *after* I had worked for a year, *then* I'd be entitled to be heard, and not until.

I filled out the endless forms in the most slipshod way, feeling the whole business of detailed record-keeping far beneath my dignity. But my dignity fell flat on its face the day the boss tacked a number of my forms on the bulletin board, with the multitudinous mistakes circled in bright red pencil. I was held up as a first-class bad example of a sloppy workman. After that, I didn't care if he ever implemented any of my good ideas or not. All I wanted was out. Surely there was another job somewhere that was big enough for my superlative abilities.

One of my friends had told me about Henry Greenberg, but I couldn't believe what I heard. The story was that Henry was just thirty-one years old and that he had already made a million dollars selling life insurance. To me, being a life insurance salesman had always seemed about the lowest occupation on the totem pole, just half a step above being a used-car salesman. I wasn't remotely interested in being either one. Still, a million dollars—

I was almost twenty-five already, and had hardly two nickels to rub together every month after the bills were paid, even though Joy and I were both working. So when Henry, whom I had never met, called me one night from his phone in his brand-new Lincoln Continental and invited me to dinner at the swankiest restaurant in Miami, I jumped at the chance.

Henry's appearance appalled me. He was short, and had an adolescent-lumpy complexion. In spite of his obviously expensive clothes, he didn't look like a millionaire. But the roll of bills in his pocket could have choked a horse. His wife, on the other hand, looked like she had stepped out of *Vogue*, and his house was a genuine mansion, overpowering even *my* imagination.

I hadn't listened to Henry for five minutes before I knew he was the most fantastic salesman I had ever heard. By the time we had finished dinner, I was sold on selling life insurance. I forgot the jokes about men in that profession. Henry had persuaded me that a Lincoln Continental, a magnificent house, and anything else I wanted that money could buy, were right around the corner for me if I would follow his instructions exactly.

The next day, I turned in my blood-testing equipment to the Miami Health Department, bequeathed to them my mountain of incomplete forms, and took a deep breath. Then I picked up the eight-minute sales presentation Henry had told me to memorize. I had tried to talk him out of requiring me to do that because memorizing was always difficult for me, and besides, I thought I could write a better presentation of my own. He was insistent that I do things his way, however, and there was a million-dollar incentive for me to follow in his footsteps.

"I have an unusual idea that many men in your . . ." I drilled the presentation over and over until I could say it in my sleep.

The presentation learned, I went out to interview my first prospect. He bought a policy from me.

I interviewed the second prospect. He bought a policy from me.

I interviewed the third prospect. He bought a policy from me.

The presentation had proved its worth. I didn't think any longer about writing up one of my own. Day after day, I approached my prospects with the infallible canned speech, "Sir, I have an unusual idea that many men in your circumstances . . ." and day after day they signed on the dotted line. By the second month, I was the leading salesman in the Miami office of the John Hancock Insurance Company, and I was winning every contest in sight. In my first six months, I sold over $500,000 worth of life insurance in a city where I knew practically nobody on the right side of the tracks.

One day the manager called me into his office and told me that the police department had called and asked if a Sid Roth was in their employ. Then the manager asked me if I had been on North

West Fortieth Street at ten o'clock the night before, knocking on doors.

"Yes," I admitted, my heart beating fast, wondering what was wrong with that.

"Well, Sid, somebody saw you and thought you must be a burglar. Life insurance salesmen don't usually go knocking on doors that late at night unless they have an appointment ahead of time."

I blushed, stammered some kind of lame-brained explanation about how I didn't realize it was so late at the time, and waited for the dressing-down that never came.

"You've got chutzpah, Sid, real chutzpah," he chuckled, genuine admiration in his voice.

Compliments always went to my head and made me more overbearing than ever. Later that day, I was chewing out a secretary who hadn't been filing my insurance applications properly. I was really giving her a hard time, my humiliating complaints about her inefficiency echoing loudly down the hall. The manager happened to hear the whole ugly bit, and called me into his office for a word of advice.

"Take it from me, Sid," he said. "You can catch more flies with honey than with vinegar."

So who wants to catch flies? I thought. I just grunted an uh huh, smiled and went back to my office. I was embarrassed that he had overheard me being so rude. Since he had just complimented me about my chutzpah, I didn't want him to see me in a bad light. I resolved to keep my voice low the next time I criticized those dumb office girls.

For the first time in my post-college career, I was making real money in a job that had an exciting future for me. But I was bored, bored almost to death, with my job, our marriage, everything.

It reminds me of a song I wrote shortly after arriving in Miami. The title was, "There Must Be Something More!" And the words went like this: "Because I work, eat, sleep and that's the way it goes, there must be something more!" In desperation something was screaming from deep within—*There must be something more!*

Chapter Ten

Thief

Whatever and wherever the something more was, it didn't seem to be in Miami. Joy was as fed up with her job there as I was with mine, and we were about fed up with each other, snarling at one another, quarrelling about everything. Life seemed to have no future; it was empty, colorless, devoid of meaning and excitement. Maybe a change of scenery would help. We took a two-weeks' vacation and headed for Washington, D.C.

The grass did look greener there, especially after the Washington branch of the Hancock Insurance Company agreed to pay all our relocation expenses if I would sell for them in D.C. The offer had everything going for it. In Miami, many of my first sales were requiring callbacks. Clients were not paying their premiums, and I was required to find out why, to resell them if necessary. I despised callbacks. If I left the Miami area, the local manager would have to take care of callbacks for me.

In addition to that, the financial future for me would surely be more promising in Washington where I knew so many people. After all, if I could sell $500,000 worth of insurance as a greenhorn in Miami, a city where I knew practically no one on the right side of the tracks, I should really be able to clean up in Washington where I had lived most of my life. And maybe Joy would be happier there, too, being able to see her parents more often. The beautiful smile that had attracted me to her in the first place had been buried under a grim hanging-on-for-dear-life look for some time now.

The only way we could ever leave Miami any time soon was to have someone foot the bill for us. I had just drained our savings account to invest in a sure-fire scheme that was taking a little longer to pay off than I had anticipated.

Another insurance salesman, my good friend, Mike Behrman, had told me about the deal where I could turn our $2,000 of savings into a cool coin collection worth at least $15,000, if I had the nerve to fork over the money and wait it out for a couple of weeks. The day I went home to get the passbook so I could withdraw the money from our savings account, Joy had given me a hard time about it.

"Sid!" she said, in her most disgusted tone when I told her what I was going to do. "Nobody in his right mind would give you a collection worth $15,000 for only $2,000. You *know* that."

I argued her out of it somehow, even though I knew that most of our savings were the result of her slaving away at a job she couldn't stand. Persuading myself that I knew best, and telling her that she'd rejoice with me when we had more money than ever, I took the passbook and emptied the account.

I gave Mike the money, in crisp new twenties, just the way he'd asked for it, got a written receipt, and his promise that he'd turn the money over to his contacts, the guys who would soon have the coins in their possession. He wasn't too explicit about exactly who *they* were, and I thought it best not to be too inquisitive. His innuendos led me to believe they were in close cahoots with the Mafia if not actually members of it themselves.

For a few weeks, I had waited patiently, without any anxiety at all, dreaming how I would spend the money after I got my hands on the coin collection and sold it for its true value. I knew, of course, that the deal wasn't strictly on the up and up, that maybe the coins were stolen property, but I couldn't afford to be too fussy about that. For a 650% profit in a few weeks' time, I expected to take *some* risk.

While I waited, Joy didn't give me any peace about it, needling me every day about when my friend was going to deliver the valuable merchandise. I gritted my teeth and said less and less about it as the weeks went by. I saw my friend every day at work, and he kept assuring me that the details were being worked out, that I shouldn't blow my cool. He made me feel appreciative that he was taking such big risks for me in his dealing with the syndicate.

One afternoon, Mike told me he had something important and confidential to discuss, so we arranged to meet at a bar after work that day. In my excited optimism, I thought he was probably going to make the pickup and delivery that day. I couldn't keep my mind on my prospects, I was so expectant. But when he walked into the bar, he didn't have anything in his hands.

"It's like this, Sid," Mike said when we had seated ourselves at a little round table in a dim corner and the waitress had brought us our drinks. "You've paid your money in good faith, the guys *mean* to keep their end of the bargain, but—"

He paused to lift his glass and drain it, and my heart slid into my shoes.

"But what?" I demanded. "There can't be any buts about it. A deal's a deal." I was amazed at how cold and hard, criminal almost, my own voice sounded.

"Now don't get uptight, Sid," Mike said, furrowing his brow and lifting his hand to stop my impatience. "There's still a way to pull the fat out of the fire. It's just going to take a little more money.

"How much?"

"Well, I'm not at liberty to divulge details, you understand—"

"Cut the explaining! Just tell me how much!" I could feel my hands tightening on my glass.

"Six hundred."

"*Six hundred!*" My whole being was outraged. "*Six hundred?*"

"Yep. Six hundred. Today. The whole shebang is down the drain unless you can come up with six hundred more. Today.

He might as well have said six thousand. I'd given him all our savings already. There wasn't another dime—but wait. There *was* one possibility. No, it was better than a possibility, it was a sure thing. I slapped the table.

"Let me make a phone call. It'll take just a sec."

I almost tipped the little table over in my haste to get to a phone. I dialed the number so familiar to me, and felt a surge of relief when Mom answered.

"Can't explain it now, Mom, but I've got to have $600 right away, today."

I heard the swift intake of her breath and could imagine the stricken look on her face as she almost wailed, "Oh, Sidney, you're not hurt, are you? Or in trouble? Nothing's wrong with my boy—"

"No, no Mom. It's just that I *have* to have six hundred right now. Look, I'll explain everything when we get to Washington next week. You'll get the money back, every penny of it, I promise. But wire it to me right now, okay?" I was almost snapping at her, right in the midst of asking such a huge favor. She had every right to turn me down, but she never had before. I waited. And then it came.

"Sure, Sidney. You want me to wire $600. I'll do it right away."

I forced a "Thanks, Mom," from my lips and hung up the phone, imagining her end of the conversation as I worked my way through the after-work crowd and back to our table. She'd be saying, "Now take care of yourself, Sidney," and then, even after she realized I'd hung up, she'd say the inevitable, "Goodbye and good luck." She'd said that to me as long as I could remember, whenever we'd parted. "Goodbye and good luck." I knew that she might be saying goodbye to her money that day without knowing it, but with luck, Mike would still be waiting for me.

Mike was waiting. For the first time, I noticed that he looked nervous, too. And I thought about the spot he was in. Oh well, he was probably getting a hefty cut for being the go-between. I'd let him worry about his end of it.

"It's okay, Mike. Everything's going to be all right," I found myself assuring him. "The six hundred is already on its way. Mom's wiring it."

"Your mom? Sending you *that* kind of money? Just like that? What'd you tell her?"

"Why, I didn't tell her anything." I didn't think anything of it, but Mike was so impressed, he seemed to forget his own worries for a moment.

"I never had a mother who would do something like that for me," he mused. And then he stared at me so intently it made me uneasy. "Do you have any idea how lucky you are, Sid? Just to ask her and she'll send it, just like that? Fantastic!" He shook his head, as if he still couldn't believe it.

"Nothing fantastic about it," I shrugged. "That's just my mom, that's all. That's how she is. She's always been that way. She'd do anything for me, even lay down her life for me if I asked her to."

The six hundred came, I gave it to Mike, and he assured me everything would be rolling smoothly from there on out. I should have the coins in my possession in a few days' time.

The day before we were expecting the movers to arrive to pack our things for Washington, Mike told me he was sorry that there had been another unforeseen hitch. I breathed easier when I learned this one wouldn't cost me anything, just a little more waiting. I wouldn't have the coins before I moved to Washington, but as soon as he could, he would personally fly the collection to me.

When I went home that day, Joy, who had already resigned

from her job, was sitting in a lawn chair behind our apartment, reading a magazine. When I broke the news to her, her face registered utter contempt and disgust. She flung her magazine down on the grass and started screaming at me—

"Sid!" she yelled, "You'll *never* have those coins, and you know it! How could you do this to me, take all the money I worked so hard for, and just throw it away like that? Any fool would know better."

People slammed open their apartment windows and stuck their heads out to see what was going on. I was afraid to look up, because I knew everybody was watching and listening to the tirade, but Joy didn't seem to care. The harder I tried to shush her, the louder she ranted.

Finally, I just turned and went back into the apartment and let her scream at the empty air. But it got to me, just the same. When she came in, she was sobbing, and I reached out to her.

"Joy, I—"

But she wouldn't listen. She stumbled into the bedroom and slammed the door.

The day after we arrived in Washington, I sent a threatening telegram to Mike, telling him I was going straight to the police if I didn't have the merchandise by the following Friday. He telephoned, tried to calm me down, told me the coins were already in his hands for me, and that I should meet him at the airport two weeks from that Friday at gate 29 at 2:04 p.m. Delivery was having to be delayed that long, he said, in order to protect me, because the feds had gotten wind of some kind of operation, and Mike and his contacts were being watched around the clock.

I was temporarily mollified, but Joy continued full of cold outrage at how I had thrown away money she felt belonged to her. Oh, well, she would sing a different tune when the profits were in my hands.

The time passed. I got to the airport half an hour early on the appointed afternoon, and seated myself in the waiting area near the gate where Mike's flight would come in. When his flight number was called, I took a firm grip on the large empty attache case I had brought to hold the coins, and stood alongside the passageway where arrivals were beginning to stream through, searching their faces for Mike. As the unfamiliar faces passed by, I kept giving myself excuses for why he wasn't the first one off the plane, and I felt pretty good, for a while.

"He probably got stuck clear at the back of the coach," I reasoned. "Most likely, he'll be the last one off." And when the last passenger had trickled through, I just figured he had missed his flight. Nothing to get excited about. Mike had never been a stickler for promptness, and he'd probably arrived at the airport too late to make it. That being the case, he'd be along on the next flight. It was due in a couple of hours, so I bought a magazine, went up to the coffeeshop and got one to go, and brought it back down to the waiting area so I wouldn't miss him when he did come.

I finished the coffee, smoked a couple of cigarettes, leafed through the pages of the magazine without seeing them, looked at my watch a blue billion times, raising it to my ear to see if it was still running, and decided I should take it to my Uncle Abe for repair the next day. No watch in good order could possibly run that slow. When the arrival of the Miami flight was announced, I about jumped out of my skin. The deplaning passengers came through, the flight was reboarded, cleared for takeoff, and still no Mike.

Maybe he was sick or something and hadn't been able to make the flight . . . Maybe he had called to let me know, but the message hadn't reached me . . . Yes, that was surely it. I dialed Joy's parents' apartment where we were staying at the time, and when Joy's mother answered, I asked if there had been a message for me.

"Why, no, Sidney," she said, probably knowing why I was calling. "Nobody has called all day—"

"Maybe your phone is out of order?" I blurted, and then blushed with the foolishness of my question. After all, my call had gotten through all right. I hung up then, almost numb with disappointment, and tried one more call.

"Mike Behrman, operator, B-e-h-r-m-a-n, in Miami, Florida." There was the usual agony of getting the operator to understand the name, getting her to understand that I didn't have his number, having to verify his address, and then the mechanical, "I'm sorry, but the number you have called is no longer in service."

I called the Miami Hancock Agency next, to see if they could tell me how to get in touch with Mike. The secretary broke it to me with crisp efficiency.

"I'm sorry, Mr. Roth. We can't help you. Mr. Behrman left us suddenly, without any explanation. No, there is no forwarding address."

I dragged out of the airport, across the street to the parking area, found my car, and drove woodenly through the traffic back to the apartment, parked, went up in the elevator, and let myself in.

"He didn't show, huh." It wasn't a question the way Joy said it. It was a defeated I-told-you-so. I almost wished she'd yell at me, give me something to fight back against, to get me out of the awful numbness of the realization that I'd been conned, completely conned. I was just like some stupid idiot who thought he had really bought the Brooklyn Bridge for fifty bucks and had stood all night on the corner in the rain waiting for the guy to come back and hand him the title to it.

CHAPTER ELEVEN

The Fortune-Teller

The two thousand was gone, and the six hundred after it. But I was on my way to make a million, and $2,600 was less than a drop in the bucket. Joy quit bugging me about it, feeling that I had suffered enough, I guess, and Mom kept building me up by talking about what an awful cruel man my ex-friend had been to bilk me of our savings in that way.

My own indignation was used up, my wounds began to heal, and my eternal optimism took over. I poured myself back into the role of becoming a millionaire in a hurry by selling life insurance.

During our first six months in Washington, I repeated my Miami success pattern, and wound up my first year in life insurance with policies worth almost a million dollars in force. I was doing so well that Joy quit her hated secretarial job and went back to school full-time to learn to be an interior designer. We had moved into our own apartment, a great relief to both of us after having been cooped up with Joy's parents for two months. We almost felt we were happy together again. But it wasn't real, and it didn't last. Soon we were back in our respective roles of merely tolerating one another's presence.

One day my Uncle Abe called, all excited about a new kind of life insurance policy that was tied in with a mutual fund. It sounded different, all right, but lousy. I told him so, and insisted that what I was selling was far superior to what anyone else had to offer. I knew that Uncle Abe had my best interests at heart, however, and I agreed to meet with him and the other agent and hear about the other guy's "superior" product.

Much to my surprise, after two hours, I agreed that his product was better than mine, and I was ready to change jobs. When I told my boss I was quitting, he was furious because not only was I quitting, but I was taking two of the best salesmen on his force with me into the new thing.

"Sid, you can't do that!" he roared. "It's against every rule of ethics! We paid to move you up here, and we've got a big investment in you and those other salesmen. We're entitled to a return on our investment!" The louder he shouted, the more right he was, the more immovable I became.

"Look," I told him, a menacing tone in my voice, "I've already contributed more than enough to this outfit. I'd be a fool not to put my own best interests first, and that goes for these other guys, too. You don't own us, you know."

After the sneering way I talked to him, it's a wonder he didn't throw me out.

During my second year in the insurance business, this time with Chatfield Associates, I sold over a million dollars worth of insurance again. By the end of the year, I was a manager with ten men under me. My sales unit was one of the top production units in the country, and hardly a week passed without a telegram congratulating me for some new sales achievement.

Somewhere along the line, after about a year and a half with Chatfield, it occurred to me that if I could sell so well for other people, I was a fool to line *their* pockets. I ought to move out on my own, start my own company, and then I'd really be bringing it in.

But my own company died aborning. Something seemed to go wrong with my selling ability, and I wasn't able to communicate it to the men I hired to work for me. The office moved too slowly, and after less than six months, I closed up shop and took a new position with another outfit. For part of a year, I worked for them as a regional manager, traveling a lot, setting up offices, and training personnel. But it went sour, too. I recognized that I was going nowhere fast, and I began looking for another position, one where they would really appreciate me. In spite of my initial success in selling life insurance, all I wanted was out.

In the midst of my job-hopping, Joy told me that we were expecting a baby. Well!

After our daughter was born, even I could see that hopping from one poorly done job to another was no way to raise a family. When I was given a chance to go to work as an executive with Merrill, Lynch, Pierce, Fenner & Smith, one of the finest investment companies in America, I recognized it as being exactly what I needed. No more peddling life insurance. Any clod could do that. This was the career spot I should have been in years ago. The sky was the limit.

After three months local training, I went to New York for more intensive instruction. During the two months I spent there, away from Joy and our baby girl, I made the rounds of the singles bars at night. I turned into a real swinger. Whatever shreds of our marriage had been left hanging together disintegrated completely.

Not because I wanted to, but out of a peculiar obedience to some kind of "ought to," I telephoned Joy from a bar on New Year's Eve. She was crying when she answered the phone, but she managed to sob out that her father, who had been an alcoholic for years, had just shot himself in the head.

Joy sounded so pitiful, so alone, so upset, that I got a cab to the airport and was on the next plane for Washington. But where I had been, and what I had become, were so sickeningly obvious to Joy when she saw me, that she told me I needn't have bothered to come home. Our marriage was finished.

Joy had had all the unfaithfulness, all the neglect, she could take from me. She wanted just one thing more. A separation.

Separation. Unthinkable for a Jewish family. When I was a child, my parents had talked seriously of separation once. My father had said that he and I would move to New York, and Shirley would stay in Washington with Mom. He promised that I'd love it in New York with him, but I couldn't imagine life without Mom fighting my battles for me, and I couldn't imagine Dad living without her, either, no matter how violently they disagreed about some things.

Somehow, they had worked out their differences, or figured how to live with them, and the split hadn't come.

As I examined my own feelings, I admitted that a part of me wanted to leave Joy, all right, but there was another part that seemed to want us to stay together in spite of everything. It was going to be a difficult decision for me to make.

For the last two years, I had been turning to a fortune-teller for help with the major decisions in my life. I would ask him what I should do.

For as long as I could remember, I had been interested in everything to do with the new age, occult, astrology, fortune-telling, handwriting analysis, reincarnation, hypnosis, communicating with the dead, spiritualism, Ouija boards, and psychic powers. All held a fascination for me that was far beyond a mere hobby or fad or interest. It was as if a supernatural force drew me, and when one of my mother's friends had told her one day about the new fortune-teller she'd discovered, and how positively fantastic he was, I was quick to get his address.

When I first went into the nondescript office building where he had his place of business, I found the fortune-teller himself to be a very solid ruddy-faced individual instead of the wraith the atmosphere of the place suggested. He was sitting behind a screen in the corner of a shabby room that served also as a waiting area for his clients, and I seated myself across the rickety card table from him. The first thing he told me, as he shuffled through his cards and fanned them out, sent chills down my spine.

"Sir, your parents live near Sixteenth Street in upper Northwest near Kennedy Street," he said, matter-of-factly.

Wow! How could he have known that? They lived just one block from Kennedy! That was near, all right. And there was no way he could have known that just from looking at me.

I was so impressed with the fortune-teller's supernatural knowledge that I consulted him about every major decision from then on. Several times, Joy and I quarreled over the fact that I couldn't seem to decide anything without consulting him first. There were periods when I visited him several times a week.

Once it occurred to me to wonder, since he had such supernatural powers, why he wasn't a millionaire in the stock market, why he didn't have a plusher office, why he needed my miserable three dollars a visit. But I quickly brushed such questioning aside. I was hooked.

When I asked the fortune-teller whether or not I should leave Joy, he gave me a strong go-ahead, and I was relieved that I didn't have to make the decision for myself.

Looking in the newspaper for a place to stay, I found a roommate referral service which put me in touch with a swinging bachelor named Jeff. His apartment was nicely furnished, immaculately clean. There was only one catch. Jeff's girl friend shared his bedroom.

"Sid, do you mind if my girl friend sleeps with me?" he asked.

"Yes," I answered. "I do mind—because she isn't sleeping with me." We laughed, and I had passed the test.

When Joy was at work the next day, I moved my clothes out of our apartment and drove off into my new, exciting, glamourous, bachelor-at-large life. Wanting to make a clean break with everything in my past, I asked the fortune-teller if it would be all right for me to change jobs again. He had always approved my job changes before, even triggered my looking for a new job sometimes by telling me that I would be changing jobs soon, but this time he turned thumbs down, advising me against leaving Merrill, Lynch. He had an elderly client who sold stocks from time to time and gave the money to him. I was a convenient broker to handle these transactions without asking foolish questions.

Still, I knew I wasn't measuring up at Merrill, Lynch, and it would be easier to start over somewhere else than to dig in and do a good job there. I didn't take the fortune-teller's advice, but jumped when a new company offered me a stock option for going with them.

Having failed to take the fortune-teller's advice, I decided not to see him again, but I felt absolutely lost without someone to turn to for guidance.

Chapter Twelve

Power Hook-Up

One day, Mike Wasserman, my assistant sales manager at Glenwood Equities, was talking to me about one of his cases. He knew I had consulted a fortune-teller in the past, and he started telling me about a friend of his who once had no fortune-telling ability of his own at all, but who had taken a mind-control course that had revolutionized his life. Now he had supernatural abilities far beyond those of any ordinary fortune-teller. He knew things about other people that he had no natural way of knowing; he knew what was going to happen in the future; he knew everything he needed to know.

Wow! That sounded like exactly what I needed. I could no longer hide the fact that my ability in business was getting shaky. My sales had no staying power, and I was losing clients right and left. My best salesmen were leaving me. All in all, I had hit a real string of bad luck. If I had some of the psychic ability Mike's friend had received from the mind-control course, maybe then I could stay on top of things. Why, with that kind of ability, I probably wouldn't even need a job!

On my next Saturday off, I drove up to New Jersey to meet Mike's friend, to give him an acid test.

"Russ," I said, getting right to the point of my visit, "your friend Mike has been telling me that the mind-control course you took enables you to tap into supernatural power so you *know* things you have no natural way of knowing. Is that right?"

"Try me," he challenged. "See for yourself. Just give me the name of someone who's had something wrong with him, and I will tell you what it is. Anyone at all."

"Gilmore Young," I said, giving him the name of Joy's father.

Russ closed his eyes, seemed to be concentrating intently, his eyelids fluttering, and said, "I see a light starting toward this man—toward his head. It's entering his head—and starting to shatter—"

Russ's eyes popped wide with wonder as he stammered, "Could this man have been shot in his head—with a bullet?"

That was all I needed to know. Russ had supernatural power all right. Just think what I could do when that power was mine!

A new mind-control class would begin in the D.C. area in a month. I marked it on my calendar, crossing off the days as it came closer and closer. I knew it would be what I had been searching for all my life, a can't-fail approach to acclaim and financial success.

If I could have known that what lay ahead was not acclaim and success, but stark terror, I'd have run screaming in the opposite direction. But I didn't know. And I would not know until after I had plunged headlong into hell.

The day finally arrived, the day when supernatural powers beyond anything I had ever observed in the fortune-teller would begin to be mine. I drove with mounting excitement to the Sheraton, where the introductory mind-control lecture would be held.

The instructor appeared to be in his middle twenties, intelligent-looking, neatly dressed. There was nothing outward to distinguish him or his twenty-odd listeners from people at a typical organization meeting. He told us that after the one-week course, we would be able to, among other things, control our weight, improve our memories, know what other people were thinking, cure illnesses, and better our finances.

It sounded too good to be true. But it had to be legitimate. There was a money-back guarantee. Anyone who couldn't demonstrate real psychic ability by passing an acid test at the end of a week would have his money refunded.

As the instructor talked on, I knew I was going to make it big. All my former failures, those I had pretended were successes, faded. It was as if my life was beginning all over again. Right, this time. Goodbye frustration and failure, spinning my wheels, going nowhere. Hello happiness, going *somewhere.*

The first two days of class, we learned how to relax. The object was to lower the speed of our brain waves to the state that occurs in sleep. After reaching this level, we were told to imagine that we had a counselor in our head. The counselor would be able to answer any questions we might ask, to perform any test we asked of him.

I listened intently to all the instructor told us, practiced relaxing to lower my brain waves, got acquainted with my counselor, and was ready for the acid test the last day of the course.

The instructor gave me the name of a woman I had never heard of. I closed my eyes, lowered my brain waves, and began to meditate. In a few moments, I saw a stick figure of a woman in my imagination. She had a large "x" over one of her breasts.

"Could she have cancer of the breast?" I blurted.

"That's right, Sid! That's right!" The instructor applauded, and the class joined him. I had passed the acid test. Supernatural power was mine.

When I went to the office the next morning, I could hardly wait to experiment with my new talent. My boss passed by my office, and I called him in, asking him to give me the name of someone I didn't know—someone who was sick. My boss looked at me as if he thought I had flipped my lid, but he gave me the name of a man.

I closed my eyes, lowered my brain waves, and suddenly, without warning, I felt my arms begin to shake.

"Why, that's exactly what my father does!" my boss exclaimed, obviously as surprised as I was.

"Could he have Parkinson's disease?" I heard myself saying. I didn't know what the disease was, nor anything about its symptoms. The name just came to me.

"Yes, that's it!" my boss said, excitedly rising from his chair. Then I told him that I didn't need to shake my arms anymore.

"That's right!" he exclaimed again. "Yesterday my father started taking a new medication, and his shaking was controlled!"

Wow! This new ability was terrific. The power seemed to be increasing all the time. Yesterday I only had visions, today I feel the symptoms. I wonder what new will happen tomorrow?

The power was real, all right. And the more I experimented, the more uses I found for it.

One afternoon, I was lost in the maze of roads winding through a park, and I said, "Counselor, direct me home." I made turns without hesitation on streets that were totally unfamiliar to me, and found myself home in record time.

If I needed a parking space, all I had to do was ask that a space be available.

It didn't matter how hard the situation was, my counselor was able to take care of it. He was even more powerful than the secret weapon of my growing-up years. There was no telling how high I would climb with all this supernatural power at my disposal.

Almost as quickly as I thought of something I wanted, and without my saying a word, people began doing my will. All I had to do was ask. I would never wait for anything again. I had found an illimitable pot of gold at the end of an unfading rainbow.

One of my first thoughts, when I realized I could have anything I wanted, was that I shouldn't work for anyone else ever again.

I should go back into business for myself. This time, I was bound to prosper.

Almost as soon as I had the thought, Jim Fisk, an attorney whom I knew only casually, just happened to drop by my office.

"Sid," he said, "I've been thinking that you just might want to go back into business for yourself. In case you do, I have some extra office space available in my building. We'd be glad to let you have it free until you get on your feet. We'll supply your phone and secretary. You might even be able to sell some stock in our company, and make some extra commissions for yourself for a starter."

After he left, I thought I'd check with my new power to see what he thought about Fisk's offer.

"Counselor, make me money," I said.

Immediately I was led to open the dictionary at random and point to a word. When I looked down, my finger was on the word "anchor." That was the name of a mutual fund company I had worked with one time in the past. I called them up, and the regional man said they would be delighted for me to open my own office and go into business representing them. Just like that. And just like that, I resigned from my job and set up shop in my free office.

Chapter Thirteen

What is the Source of Your Power?

At the time I set up my own office, I was ignorant of the fact that Jim Fisk, the president of the computer company that gave me the free space, was a Bible believer. That was bad enough, but even worse, Jim had all the "Jesus people" in town trooping through his offices, and they had prayer meetings morning, noon, and night.

Somehow, although I thought they were all kooks, I liked them. They were more than nice to me, projecting a kind of love and acceptance I had never seen before. And they did it even though they didn't approve of my mind-control involvement. Well, I was glad *they* had that kind of love, but it wasn't for me.

Soon after I had moved into my new free office, I met Art Lane. He was tall, well-built, distinguished-looking with prematurely gray hair, and very articulate. Art had every quality a man of the world ought to have, and I came to admire him greatly. But there was something strange about him. Although Art was a Jew, he attended the Bible studies with the Gentile guys in the office building. I couldn't understand why a Jew would be studying the

Scriptures with a bunch of Gentiles. It didn't make sense, but it did arouse my curiosity, so I began attending the sessions, too.

I gave them a hard time, questioning everything they said, ridiculing their faith. But they didn't throw me out. They didn't even give me harsh answers. Gradually it dawned on me that they were praying for me! That made me laugh. It was utterly ridiculous. But if it suited them, let them go ahead. I was glad for my free office and the friendship that gave and gave and gave without requiring anything from me.

One day Art Lane stopped by my office to talk about the insurance business. We talked about other things, too. He told me that he himself had come to "know the Lord" through reading the Hebrew Scriptures and understanding that Yeshua—Hebrew for Jesus—was the One who had fulfilled all the prophecies about the coming Messiah. Then he asked me a question.

"Sid, do you have a Bible?"

"Well, no," I admitted.

"I'll bring you one the next time I drop by," he promised. "But in the meantime—"

Art opened his Bible and showed me some Scriptures telling about the Messiah who was to come, and some additional Scriptures in the New Covenant that showed that a Jew named Yeshua had fulfilled every single Messianic prophecy.

I was bored with the whole business. "Look, Art," I interrupted, "if the Messiah had already come, the rabbi in our synagogue would surely have told us all about it—"

"Oh, but that's part of the prophecy, too, Sid," Art smiled. Then he pointed to some verses in the book of the prophet Isaiah, and I read: "Who would have believed our report? and to whom is the arm of the Lord revealed? . . . He was despised and rejected of men . . . and we esteemed him not."

"You see, Sid," Art went on, "if we Jews had *received* Yeshua when He came, He would not have been the Messiah.

With that intriguing remark hanging in the air, Art left my office. But the gleam in his eye warned me that he was in league with the Bible believers who were praying for me.

Well, they could pray all they wanted. But I was quite satisfied with my own life, thank you. Being separated from my wife, I had freedom to come and go as I pleased, and with my fast-growing mind-control powers, I would soon have the material world on a string. If there *was* a Messiah, I didn't need Him for anything.

Another of the men in the office building who attended the Bible-study prayer meetings was Gene Griffin. He was an inventor who had spent a year in a kibbutz, a community farm, in Israel. I thought it strange that a Gentile would take a year out of his life just to help Israel. And I noticed something else strange about Gene. He didn't act like a businessman or an inventor. It seemed that every time I looked at him, he was reading the Bible.

"You know, Sid," Gene said to me one day, "your God, the God of Abraham, and Isaac, and Jacob, is not pleased with your involvement in mind control. He condemns all new age, occult practices."

"What do you know about my God?" I challenged.

"Plenty," he assured me. "Because there's only one God. My God is the same as your God. And if you'll read the eighteenth chapter of Deuteronomy in your own Tanakh, your Jewish Bible, especially the ninth through the twelfth verses, God's opinion about the occult will be plain to you."

I picked up the Bible Art had given me a few days previously, thumbed to Deuteronomy and read:

> *When thou art come into the land which the* LORD *thy God giveth thee, thou shalt not learn to do after the abominations of those nations. There shall not be found among you any one that maketh his son or his daughter to pass through the fire, or that useth divination, or an observer of times, or an*

> *enchanter, or a witch, or a charmer, or a consulter with familiar spirits, or a wizard, or a necromancer. For all that do these things are an abomination to the* LORD . . . (KJV).

Talk about relevance! The Scripture made it sound as if reading my horoscope (observer of times), visiting my fortune-teller (divination), and consulting my counselor, or channeling (consulting with familiar spirits) were things not pleasing to God. They were actually abominations! But what was this "necromancer?" I looked it up in the dictionary. It meant to communicate with the dead.

So seances are wrong? What about reincarnation?

Gene said, "Those who claim to be reincarnated and those who communicate 'from the dead' at seances are not our loved ones, but are familiar spirits who know everything about our deceased loved ones. They even know the events of history because they existed during those events.

"These spirits are looking for a body to inhabit. That's how channeling really operates.

"Reincarnation and the laws of karma say you keep coming back until you are perfect. The Bible says '. . . man is destined to die once, and after that to face judgment' (Heb. 9:27).

"Even if you could come back, it would not make you righteous. We only become righteous when we receive the free gift of the Messiah's righteousness. A true Christian or Messianic Jew will never be more righteous than at the moment he makes Yeshua Lord. We are '. . . the righteousness of God in him' (2 Cor. 5:21b, KJV). And you can't get any more righteous than that!"

"Aw, that can't mean what you think it does." I told Gene, closing the book. "Just like I've been telling you guys, God's in charge of all knowledge. Why, He probably *wants* us to explore every avenue of knowledge—supernatural, natural, the whole bit. Everything we can learn about good *or* evil is to our benefit."

"Ever hear what happened to Adam and Eve when they nibbled at the fruit of the tree of the knowledge of good and evil?" he asked.

"Fer cryin' out loud! How naive can you get!" I exploded. "Don't you guys realize that these things have been handed down and handed down from one generation to the next? There are many difficulties in translating any language; and probably so many errors have crept in the Scriptures that what they say now isn't even remotely related to what the original said."

I didn't realize I had been shouting until Gene answered me in a super-soft voice, telling me that God had protected the authenticity of the Bible in supernatural ways. But I wasn't buying any of that.

The next afternoon, I was trying to talk Jim Fisk into digging into his subconscious mind through mind control. Apparently he had had more than enough of my hassling because after a while, he put his hands over his ears. When I took the hint and shut up, he let me have it.

"Look, Sid. I don't want to talk to you anymore about it. I don't want to argue with you. I can't handle it. Tell you what you can do. You won't take my word for anything, you won't take the Bible's word for anything. So okay. But why don't you ask God who Jesus is?" With that, he strode out of the office.

I hadn't told Jim I would ask God about that, but it was an interesting question to think about. I wondered what God would tell me if did I ask Him. But God had never told me anything before. And I wasn't in the habit of asking Him anything.

"Look," I told myself, "I'll accept that this Jesus was a man, a real historic figure. And He probably was a good teacher, lived a moral and upright life—

"But if that's all He was," I interrupted myself, "why are people so all-fired excited about Him two thousand years later, just as if He's still alive?"

That was another interesting question. But it hung in the air, unanswered and unanswerable.

At that moment, I happened to notice a little white leaflet parked on the corner of my desk. Jim Fisk had handed it to me one day. I had flipped through without reading it, and had put it down on my desk where it had rested, undisturbed. For some reason, I picked up the leaflet now, and began reading.

"Have you heard of the four spiritual laws?" the cover asked. I hadn't, so I read on.

The leaflet was simple, easy to read. The first law said that God loved me and that He had a plan for my life. Well, that was all right. I had a plan for my life, too; I wanted to be famous and rich. God's plan couldn't beat that.

The second law said that man is sinful and separated from God. And the punishment for sin was eternal separation from God at death with no chance of reversing it. Then the third law said that Jesus, Yeshua in Hebrew, was God's remedy for man's sin and separation from Him. Yeshua lived a perfect life and died as my substitute. The fourth law said that in order for a man to have this substitution, he had to "receive Jesus . . . by personal invitation."

After the four spiritual laws had been explained, there was a page with a prayer on it that a person could pray to invite this Jesus to live inside of him.

I wasn't really interested in doing that, but I figured it couldn't hurt anything, so just sitting there in my chair, I read the prayer aloud, very softly so that if anyone happened to come in, they wouldn't know what I was up to:

> *Lord Jesus, forgive my sins. I'm sorry. I open the door of my life and receive you as my Savior and Lord. Live inside of me. Take control of the throne of my life. Make me the kind of person you want me to be. Thank you for coming into my life and for hearing my prayer as you promised.*

That was all there was to it. When I had finished reading the prayer, I didn't feel any different. No lights flashed, I didn't hear anything. And I figured the prayer hadn't "worked." Well, that was perfectly all right with me. I had just read it for kicks anyway. I had known all along that there wasn't anything to all this Jesus business, and now I was satisfied that I had proved it. But there was something supernatural about that prayer, and despite not feeling anything, God now had access to my life.

At quitting time that afternoon, Gene Griffin stuck his head in the door, breaking into my thoughts with a startling question.

"Sid, if God says that all who dabble in the occult are an abomination to Him, guess where your supernatural power is coming from?"

Gene just stood there, waiting for my answer. But I didn't have one! Where was the power coming from?

Fear hit me for a split second. Was there a devil? Could I be in league with him? Could the devil be the source of my power in mind control?

It couldn't be. That bit about the devil was just superstitious nonsense. I snapped back to my senses.

"Look, Gene. Like I told you. I don't believe the Bible we have today is the Bible God wrote originally. Man has changed it over the centuries. And there probably isn't such a thing as the devil."

Gene didn't answer. He just smiled and slipped quietly from my office, leaving me to argue with myself.

Even though I didn't understand all of that Deuteronomy scripture and I wasn't sure the Bible was the Word of God, the thought that I might be in league with the devil was planted in my mind, and it began to grow.

I decided to get the answer from the mind-control people themselves. I would ask them where the power was coming from. They would know.

That night I went to see my local instructor.

"Bill, just where does this power we use in mind control come from?"

"Search me, Sid," he said. "I don't know. I've never given it any thought, actually."

He didn't know! The man who had tapped me into my counselor didn't know where the power came from!

Bill saw the fear in my face.

"Sid, maybe you'd better not take the advanced course," he suggested. "I'll refund your money. But if you really want an answer to your question, I'll arrange a meeting for you with the top instructor in mind control in the country."

I jumped at the offer. The meeting was scheduled for two weeks from that day, in Harrisburg, Pennsylvania.

I could hardly wait to tell Gene about it. "You and your friends and your Bible can go with me to Harrisburg," I said, planning it all out in my mind. "You can sit on one side of the table and the mind-control man on the other. I'll sit in the middle, and may the best power win."

But Gene said he'd have to pray about it first, and after he had prayed, he told me that God didn't want him to go to the meeting with me. I exploded. That messed up my beautiful plan, and when the day came, I found myself on the road to Harrisburg, feeling more foolish with every passing mile. I felt as if I was taking the trip to defend the Bible, a book I didn't even believe in.

When I was seated across a luncheon table from the instructor, we talked about everything except the burning subject until the waitress brought our dessert. I began by asking, "What do you think of evil?"

He laughed at the foolishness of my question before he dismissed it with an unequivocal answer, "There's no such thing as evil." He was so cocksure, I knew he had to be right. How humiliating it would be to argue with someone who spoke with such authority.

Almost apologetically, I showed him the Bible and asked him what he thought about it. He smiled and said, "It's a good book, but there are lots of good books." His manner suggested that any fool would know that.

To my great relief, before I could ask him anything else, he called for his check and said he had to be going. His parting remark was, "By the way, Mr. Roth, the next time you want to ask me something, no need to drive all these miles to do it. Don't pick up your telephone either. Just address your thoughts to me, and I'll pick them up and send your answers back, mind to mind. Cheaper than postage, you know, and a whole lot faster service." He slid a tip under the edge of his plate, strode to the cash register and then out of the restaurant.

I just sat there with my mouth hanging open. Boy! Think of how tremendous *his* powers were. Just wait until mine were that developed!

Mind control was really the thing. I would stop listening to my kooky religious friends who were trying to scare me out of using it. They could stay back in the boondocks if they wanted. I would get ahead with *my* life.

Chapter Fourteen

Seed of Fear

At the next mind-control meeting I attended, someone told me that a friend of his had used his mind-control powers on a jockey at a horse race, causing him to fall from his horse, and nearly get killed. The accident let the mind-control guy's nag win the race! *Wow, that's power*, I thought.

But some long-dormant vestige of conscience in me bristled at the thought that mind-control power could be used to hurt somebody. I had been told it could only be used for good.

At the same meeting, some of the more advanced students were asking their counselors what they would be doing in the future. I asked the most advanced student what his counselor saw me doing a year from now.

"Just a minute, Sid, and I'll find out," he said. He closed his eyes, lowered his brain waves, and almost immediately his eyes flew open. There was a startled look on his face.

"Sid, I don't understand. My counselor has always been a perfect gentleman with me, but when I asked him what you would be doing a year from today, he started cursing and using all kinds of vulgarity. And he refused to answer my question."

The instructor had no explanation for this strange kind of

behavior from a counselor. He'd never encountered such a thing before, he said. What was wrong? Did the counselor see something so horrible he couldn't mention it? The seed of fear in me began to sprout and push upward.

At another meeting, a few days later, the whole class went into deep meditation. Something new happened! I saw myself come out of myself!

I was so excited, I came out of my meditation and breathlessly told the woman next to me about it.

"Oh, Sid," she said, "I'm so happy for you! You have just found your astral soul. Now you can *really* have everything you want, greater power than you ever dreamed."

For a few moments, I sat there, quietly exulting in the fact that nothing would be beyond my reach. But then I felt her hand on my arm.

"But Sid, let me warn you about something. Never let your astral soul take you too far from your body. You might not be able to find your way back."

"Not be able to find my way back?" I could feel the gooseflesh rising on my arms. "But that would mean—that would mean—I'd be dead—if my body was in one place and my soul in another—" I stammered. She nodded gravely, closed her eyes, and went back into her meditative state.

The seed of fear that had sprouted was growing in me. I shoved it down, rubbed my arms to make the gooseflesh go away, and resolved to be careful not to go too far from my body. The sensible thing was to keep my body in full view at all times. That way, I could always find my way back. Satisfied that such a precaution would be sufficient to prevent anything bad from happening to me, I continued to exercise my powers.

At a mind-control meeting the next week, the subject of astral projection came up again. The instructor explained that every time we sleep, our astral soul goes for a walk.

I nearly fell out of my chair. The pricklings of fright were chilling my flesh again. When I was awake, I could control my comings and goings, but how could I do so when I was asleep?

I shook my head, trying to clear it of my gruesome imaginings. After all, I wasn't asleep. I *was* awake. I was in *perfect* control of myself.

The next morning at the office, I had an urge to do my dictionary trick again, this time without asking a specific question in advance. I opened the book, wrote down the first word my finger pointed to, closed the book, opened it at random again, and continued the process until I had five words written on a piece of paper. I did a double take when I realized that they made a sentence: "Refrain from this sinful dictionary."

Where was *that* advice coming from? I crumpled the paper, flung it in the wastebasket, and pretended to return to the work on my desk. But the disquiet inside me wouldn't settle down, wouldn't be still. I was seething with some kind of spiritual distress, something I had never felt before.

When Gene walked into my office a few minutes later, I told him what had happened, and how I was feeling. To my surprise, he didn't try to comfort me, he just threw his hands into the air and began to laugh and praise God for His goodness. That didn't make me feel any better. Next, Jim Fisk walked in to see what all the racket was about. When Gene told him, Jim looked long and hard at me and said, "Sid, you look like you have a bad case of spiritual neurosis." Then he winked at Gene, and made a victory sign, saying, "Looks like Sid's about ready for his breakdown, huh?"

Jim was obviously needling me. What were they doing? Were they trying to crowd me into some kind of hysteria or something?

For a moment there flashed through my mind the treatment I had given Chuck Hoffman way back in "Hootenanny" days, and for the first time, I felt an uncomfortable flood of remorse about what I had done to him.

The office was getting unbearable for me. I had to get out, so I threw some papers in a briefcase and got out as fast as I could.

Could it be that my Bible-believing friends were right? Was there really a devil? By my involvement in the new age, had I cast my lot with him?

Chapter Fifteen

Out of the Pit

As I backed my car out of the parking area, I kept getting flashes of incidents in my past, all ugly ones.

My childhood tantrum on the train, racing around the table to get away from my father, copping out on my paper route, tattling, lying, cheating in school, refusing to staple letters together, leaving snarls of improperly done work behind me in more job changes than I could count, always trying to get something for nothing, profiting at the other fellow's expense, being unfaithful to Joy and thinking I was so smart to get by with it . . .

That was the afternoon of increasing terror. That was the night I went to bed with the mezuzah around my neck, the Bible under my pillow, fear enveloping me, and a broken heart inside me. That was the night I prayed to the God of Abraham, Isaac, and Jacob and asked Him to help me. That was the night I asked Joy to entreat her God in my behalf.

When I was a child I tried to imagine what death would be like. Since we never discussed death in our family, I concluded that life must end in nothingness. But that concept was so objectionable I did the only sensible thing: I stopped thinking about it.

Until now. For the first time in my life, the nothingness of death looked better than continuing a tortured existence. And with that thought I fell asleep from sheer exhaustion.

The next thing I knew, it was morning. Sunshine streamed through my window and woke me up. I was alive, really alive. The fear was gone, the counselor gone, and in its place was an indescribable joy.

I knew that Jesus was responsible. There was a greater power in his Name than in all the forces of darkness that were trying to destroy me! I knew this deep within my being.

It was just as God had promised:

> *I will give you a new heart and put a new spirit in you; I will remove from you your heart of stone and give you a heart of flesh. And I will put my Spirit in you and move you to follow my decrees and be careful to keep my laws* (Ezek. 36:26, 27).

I was free at last. And I was grateful, very grateful.

Chapter Sixteen

A Gracious Life

Even before I began to read the Scriptures about God's desires for marriage, He had been gently telling me to return to my wife and child.

I knew it was His will for me to be reconciled to my wife. We had been seeing one another frequently, and she had sensed a profound change in me. She saw that I was concerned about her, whereas before I had been utterly and unbelievably selfish. Joy told me that during the night when I had been about to die with fear, she had slipped from her bed to say a prayer for the first time in many years.

"God," she had prayed, "if You're there, please help Sid." That was all, but He had heard. And Joy saw that He had answered.

As the weeks rolled by, I became aware of His guiding my every step, just as I had asked Him to do when, without faith, that day in my office, I had read the prayer that invited Him to take charge of me.

Before many days had passed, Joy and I were living together again, and our little daughter, Leigh, had a mother and a father to love her. The things of the world that had had such a stranglehold on my attention no longer interested me. I yearned to know more about God and His plan for my life, and I thanked Him continually for my narrow escape from the forces of darkness to which I had opened my life through my involvement in fortune-telling, horoscopes, and mind control.

I wanted to warn everyone that there are two supernatural powers at work in the world, the power from God and the other, which comes disguised as enlightenment, but is laced through and through with evil. No wonder all occult involvement is an abomination to God. It is Satan's instrument to steal, kill, and destroy the very creatures for whom the Messiah died that they might have eternal life.

I soon began to receive invitations to speak to groups all over the country. After telling my story, I would see others who were in occult bondage renounce Satan and invite God to take over their lives. I watched in amazement as I saw God working.

One day, I had the joy of seeing my sister Shirley and her husband, Marc, accept the Messiah, as my friend, Don Tobias, led them in prayer. With Marc, however, the new commitment was short-lived. The next morning Marc telephoned me and took it all back.

"Look, Sid, I know that you needed the Messiah, because your life was all messed up. You were separated from Joy and mixed up in the occult and all that. But for me, well, it's different. I must have been hypnotized when I said what I did last night. There was no reason for me to do it. I have everything I need. I'm happy with my wife, have a good job, and I just don't need this in my life."

Before I could offer any arguments, he went on, "I'm going back to the way I was before. I don't need Jesus." Then he hung up.

But Shirley held to her commitment. I was confident that as she lived her new life where Marc could see it, he would reconsider his choice. God would ultimately accomplish His purpose in Marc.

Sooner than we could have guessed, Marc saw how needy he really was.

It happened one night about a year after Marc's abortive decision. I had just finished speaking to a group and was standing at the front of the auditorium, praying for a woman who had deep problems. Suddenly, I was aware of someone at my elbow, tugging at my coat.

"Sid there's an urgent phone call for you."

I ran to the telephone across the hall. The voice at the other end was incoherently sobbing something about a dead baby.

"Oh my God, not Leigh," I blurted, thinking of my own little girl.

"No. It's Cheryl Ann," the voice managed, and I realized I was talking to my sister Shirley. Her baby girl was not quite two years old.

"Marc found her," Shirley choked out. "Pulled her out of the swimming pool. Oh, Sid, the doctors say she's gone. But—when the Messiah was here on earth—" Quavering determination was in her voice now, and an urgent pleading.

"Sid, He brought the dead back to life—Oh, Sid, do you think—would He—?

"Keep praying, Shirley. Hold on. I'll come."

The folks at the meeting began to pray for Cheryl Ann, while I sped to the hospital where Shirley and Marc were waiting, hope mingled with hopelessness in their tear-swollen eyes.

Cheryl Ann was lying deathly still on a white-sheeted bed. A futile mechanical respirator was shoved into a corner. I thought, "If God performs this miracle, my whole family will become believers."

Kneeling beside the bed, my hands on Cheryl Ann's tiny chest, I prayed for a long time. Others came in to join me from time to time—a Protestant minister, a Catholic nun, a black orderly. None of them seemed shocked that I was asking God to raise the baby from the dead.

Suddenly I heard a little sound that was not my own voice nor that of any of the other prayers. Opening my eyes, I saw bubbles coming from Cheryl Ann's nostrils!

"She's alive!" I shouted, and ran to the hallway to get the nurse who had just left the room.

"I'm sorry," she said, returning to the room with me. "Those bubbles don't mean that she's alive. That often happens when someone has drowned. It's just carbon dioxide coming out of the lungs."

The nurse went out again. I prayed a little while longer, and gradually I felt the peace of God replace my anguished striving. I bent to kiss Cheryl good-bye, and thanked God that He had remained in charge and that my little niece was safe in His arms.

The next morning, Shirley called to say, "Sid, I can cope with this because of Yeshua. But Marc is almost out of his mind. He can't stand it. He's going to pieces."

As I drove to their house, I praised God for the peace He had given Shirley, and I prayed that Marc would have it too.

When I arrived, two neighbors who were in the living room with Marc left almost immediately. Marc had been struggling to keep his composure, but as soon as they were out the door, he gave way to racking sobs. I had asked God to help me say the right words, but I didn't have to say anything. I waited, praying softly, and Marc finally gathered his voice to speak. It came in an urgent whisper.

"Sid, I need help. Would your Yeshua help me?"

I nodded, and we went to his bedroom where he knelt alongside the bed and surrendered to Yeshua.

"Oh, Sid!" he exclaimed, his eyes widening, his hand spread on his chest. "It's like all the hard, heavy weight has been lifted from my heart! The pain and all that agony. It's gone! I feel something. It's—it's like a cloud of love all over me!"

We began to laugh, with joy.

"It's the Lord, Marc," I said, and he knew I spoke the truth.

Shirley had a new husband. I had a new brother. God had a new son.

At the funeral the next day, all their relatives were astounded at how well Shirley and Marc were taking the tragedy. Uncle Abe came up to me, shaking his head.

"Sid," he said, "I can't get over it—how brave they are. Shirley and Marc are putting up such a front, acting strong for the sake of the family."

"It's not a front, Uncle Abe," I told him. "It's real. Their strength comes from the Messiah who lives inside them."

He looked at me, tears streaming, and shook his head as if he thought I was crazy. I didn't say anything more, but I knew that a seed had been planted.

Cheryl's four-year-old brother, Brian, summed up a lot of things when he said to his mother, "Mommy, now that Cheryl is in heaven, we're bigger, aren't we?"

"No," Shirley said, getting down on her knees to hug him, not understanding what he meant. You mean we're smaller. We have a smaller family now."

"No, Mommy," Brian persisted, his dark eyes searching the depths of hers. "We're bigger because we all have God inside of us."

One week later, Marc and Shirley accompanied Joy and me to a Kathryn Kuhlman service in Pittsburgh, and Marc gave his testimony before a large congregation in the auditorium as well as to a huge television audience:

"I'm Jewish. I was raised in a Jewish home. We believed in God, and hoped that the Messiah would come someday. . . . But just last week, our twenty-one-month-old daughter, Cheryl Ann, was drowned in the swimming pool in our own backyard.

"We had always thought she was an angel, sent from heaven. She gave joy to so many people.

"It was hard, so hard that I couldn't wait any longer for a Messiah who might come sometime in the future. I needed a Messiah now. And in my great need, my eyes were opened to the truth that the Messiah Yeshua, the Lord Jesus, had already come, fulfilling all the prophecies in the Hebrew Scriptures.

I invited that Messiah to come into my heart, and He did, lifting the burden of sorrow that was too great for me to bear. . . .

"God gave us Cheryl Ann—her name means 'gracious life' in Hebrew—to open the gates to everlasting life for our whole family. Cheryl Ann will be waiting for us in eternity. . . ."

When Marc had finished talking, a great throng of people rose from their seats and came to the front of the auditorium. Their eyes had been opened, too, and they wanted to invite the Messiah to take over their lives.

CHAPTER SEVENTEEN

Joy in the Morning

With so many wonderful things going on all around us, I thought my wife would surely become a real believer. But somehow, it wasn't working out that way. I was so busy with my business, with speaking engagements all over the country, accelerated by several television appearances, that I was blind to how Joy was receiving it all. I wasn't even aware that I was leaving her and Leigh alone night after night until God used her to open my eyes.

One night I didn't get home until well after midnight. I tiptoed in, expecting to find Joy asleep. But she was sitting up in bed, waiting for me.

The confrontation began softly, but it didn't stay that way.

"Sidney!" she said, in a tone of voice I hadn't heard for a long time, "do you have any idea what time it is? Do you realize that you've been gone every single weekend for a month, plus two or three nights during the week? You know how much I hate to be alone all the time! It's almost like being separated again!"

"But Joy, you know all this is for the Lord!" Was there something more than a hint of self-righteousness in my defense?

"For the Lord?" she screamed. "I thought the Lord said that

husbands were to *love* their wives, not to leave them all the time. You call that love?"

I kept trying to defend myself, she kept whacking at my defenses, getting louder and more shrill.

"Shhh! You'll wake up Leigh," I cautioned, trying to calm her, but that just made her madder than ever. In her exasperation, she picked up her pillow and started hitting me with it. Other things began flying through the air, and when a book from her bedside table narrowly missed my head, I finally heard, really heard, what she was saying: I could not serve God to the neglect of my family. I began to recognize how much my ego fed on my popularity and importance with all those needy people at all those meetings. But I was needy, too—I needed to grow up.

In the meantime, some of the girls who worked with Joy in her office were becoming believers in Jesus, and were bombarding her with their experiences. They only compounded her defensiveness.

It was about this time that we signed up to go on a tour of Israel. Joy was all for it at first, because she loved to travel, and neither of us had been overseas before.

Almost all of the 150 people on the tour were real born again believers—except Joy. She became utterly exhausted by so many people talking to her about Jesus all the time. Instead of blessing her, all the talk came through as condemnation, and naturally, she blamed me.

I hadn't yet learned that it is the Spirit of God who draws people to Himself, and that our crowding overexuberance stood squarely in the way of His work.

One day Joy, sick of the whole tour group, especially me, left us to do some sightseeing on her own. Her cab driver, a Jewish man who spoke English with a heavy New York accent, was glad enough to take Joy to see the museum of the six million Jews annihilated during the Second World War, and anything that had to do with the Old Covenant. But she had a hard time persuading him to take her to see anything that had to do with Jesus.

When, late in the afternoon, she finally persuaded him to take her to the Garden Tomb, the gates had been closed.

She was angry at the cab driver, at me . . . at *everyone.* My great plans to reach Joy in Israel crashed around me.

After we returned from Israel, Joy still went to meetings of Bible believers—for my sake—but it wasn't until she went to a Messianic Jewish congregation (a congregation in which Jews and Gentiles worship God within a Jewish cultural framework and context) that her faith was challenged to make Yeshua her Lord. There, Joy heard the predictions from the Bible about Israel and Yeshua. She couldn't deny their amazing accuracy, and so it was that this Southern Baptist "atheist," who converted to Judaism for the sake of our marriage, was circumcised in her heart and became a true Jew.

Chapter Eighteen

Think For Yourself

My mother, a great peacemaker, convinced my father that my newfound belief in Jesus was a phase and it too would pass. I was very concerned for my parents' salvation and tried to witness at every opportunity. My mother would listen, but my father would get angry and close his ears. Over the years my parents watched how my marriage was restored. They observed the new stability in my life. They could see I was becoming a real mensch (Hebrew word that, roughly translated, means "a good human"). They watched my wife, daughter, sister, brother-in-law and nephews become believers. When my sister lost her daughter, Cheryl Ann, my parents observed her inner strength in dealing with this tragedy—a strength that she had not had previously.

My father was not even willing to let me talk about Messiah Jesus. After much prayer, however, he let me read to him the 53rd chapter of Isaiah. By the time I finished he was angry and accused me of reading from a Christian Bible[1] because I was reading about

[1]The major difference between a Jewish Bible and a Christian Bible is that the latter includes the New Testament. Also, the books of the Jewish Bible are in slightly different order and sometimes the verse number is different by one verse. For instance, Micah 5:2 is 5:1 in the Jewish Bible. The actual translation is essentially the same.

Jesus. I showed him it was published by the Hebrew Publishing Company, but that was not good enough. He said he would only accept a Bible from his orthodox rabbi. "Hmm," I thought, "My father thinks Isaiah is speaking of Jesus."

So the next day I called our family rabbi for an appointment. When I entered his office, he greeted me with a warm welcome and asked what he could do for me. I asked if he would give me a Bible and inscribe something personal to me. He gladly complied, writing some kind words to me on the inside cover.

I thanked him and left quickly. I could not wait to show this powerful gift to my father. When I arrived, I confidently showed my dad the inscription and made sure he read it. Then I began to read the same passage from Isaiah. Now he had only two choices. Either he had to agree Jesus was the Messiah or he had to think something was wrong with the rabbi. To my shock, he said, "I've always thought there was something wrong with that rabbi." And then he proceeded to tell me how he once saw the rabbi eating out in a restaurant on Yom Kippur—the day of fasting.

One afternoon when I went over to my parents' house for a visit, my father was at the race-track. I decided this was the time to prove to my mother that Jesus was the Messiah. I knew that she had very little knowledge of the Scriptures, did not know if they were true, and gave no thought to an after-life, although she came from a religious family and attended an orthodox synagogue.

I started by trying to prove there is a God and the Bible is His book. "Mom, did you know the entire history of the Jewish people—past, present and future—is in the Bible? Hundreds of precise predictions have come true already. And the scientific dating of the Dead Sea Scrolls in Israel proves no one entered these predictions in the Bible after the event occurred.

"For instance, God said He would bless us beyond any people that have ever lived, if we would be obedient to His laws (Deut. 28:1). However, if we disobeyed, we would lose our country, be persecuted and scattered to the four corners of the earth (Deut. 28:36,37; Is.11:12). And wherever we would flee, we would be persecuted (Deut. 28:65). And, even though many of us would suffer and die, we would always be preserved as a distinct people (Jer. 31:36). With the suffering we have gone through as Jews, you would think every Jew left alive would have assimilated, as a means of self preservation. But against impossible odds, God has preserved us as a distinct people.

"Then, in the last days a miracle would happen. Israel would become a Jewish nation (Jer. 16:15). If there were no Israel and the U.N. had to vote on it becoming a Jewish homeland today, what would the probability be? Zero would be too generous. That is how impossible it was in 1948. But God caused a great sign to occur that was of far greater magnitude than the crossing of the Red Sea as though it were dry land (Jer.16:14,15). And a nation, Israel, was formed in a day, as Isaiah predicted (Is. 66:8).

"Amos said once we returned we would *rebuild* the waste cities (Amos 9:14). And, if you investigate the history of Israel, you will find one city is built upon another. Tel Aviv is as modern and cosmopolitan as any city in the world. Isaiah even said the desert would blossom as the rose (Is. 35:1). By the way, did you know Israel exports more *roses* to Europe than any other nation? Ezekiel prophesied the reforestation of Israel (Ezek. 36:8). And Isaiah 35:7 tells us, 'The burning sand will become a pool, the thirsty ground bubbling springs.' How did Isaiah know 2,700 years ago that Israel would develop technology that would cause underground water to bubble to the surface supporting the growth of vegetation in the barren desert? Since this water originates from deep within the earth, it comes out warm, allowing growth in any weather![2]

"The only way Isaiah or any of the other prophets could have

---

[2]From an interview with Dr. Dov Pasternack of the Ben Gurion University of the Negev on "Report to Zion" Messianic Vision radio broadcast #8 (broadcast April 1989).

known these things is if God told them. Two hundred years before Cyrus was born, Isaiah 45:13 identifies him by name and says God would use this Gentile to build the Jewish Temple and restore the cities in Israel. How did Isaiah know his name? And better still, how did God get a heathen to want to restore Jerusalem? Jeremiah prophesied that Israel would go into captivity in Babylon for exactly 70 years (Jer.29:10). Guess how many years we were captive in Babylon? Mom, I could go on and on about the amazing predictions of the Bible that were written thousands of years before the fact, but would you like to know about our future? Since God has demonstrated 100 percent accuracy so far, it is reasonable to expect Him to know our future."

As I quickly moved from Scripture to Scripture, I could tell my mother was impressed with my knowledge of the Bible. And for the first time in her life she was confronted with the accuracy of the Scriptures.

"Mom, Zechariah says that in the last days the whole world will not know what to do with Jerusalem (12:3). Today, the problems of Jerusalem and the tiny nation of Israel are in the news continuously. And Israel will be invaded by many nations. The invading powers are mentioned by name (Ezek. 38:3–9). It will be a real blood bath; two-thirds of our people will perish (Zech. 13:8). And when there is no hope left, the Messiah will fight for Israel. Let me read it to you from Zechariah:

> *Then the Lord will go out and fight against those nations, as he fights in the day of battle . . . . "They [the Jewish people] will look on me, the one they have pierced, and mourn for him as one mourns for an only child, and grieve bitterly for him as one grieves for a firstborn son. On that day the weeping in Jerusalem will be great . . .* " (14:3; 12:10, 11).

"Mom, do you know why we will be weeping?" I think this

was the first time I paused for air and gave her a chance to speak.

"I guess because we will be so grateful for being spared," she said.

"That is partially right. But the main reason is that we will realize, for the first time, that Jesus is our Messiah, and we missed Him."

"But if Jesus is the Messiah why don't all the rabbis believe? Sidney, I love you, but you still don't know as much as the rabbis who have studied all their life."

"Mom, the Talmud tells us that years ago, when the rabbis pondered how to recognize the Messiah, they concluded that there would be two Messiahs. One would suffer for the people and be like Joseph. He would be rejected by his own people. He is described in Isaiah 53:

> *He was despised and rejected by men, a man of sorrows, and familiar with suffering. Like one from whom men hide their faces he was despised, and we esteemed him not* (v.3).

"And, according to Daniel 9:26, He would die before the second Temple was destroyed:

> *After the sixty-two 'sevens,' the Anointed One* [the Messiah] *will be cut off and will have nothing. The people of the ruler who will come will destroy the city and the sanctuary.*

"He would die by crucifixion. David describes this hundreds of years before the first recorded crucifixion. David even saw the guards gambling for his clothes. And he noted that His bones would not be broken because this is the requirement for acceptable sacrifices.

> *I am poured out like water, and all my bones are out of joint. My heart has turned to wax; it has melted away within me.*

> *My strength is dried up like a potsherd, and my tongue sticks to the roof of my mouth; you lay me in the dust of death . . . . They have pierced my hands and my feet. I can count* all my bones; *people stare and gloat over me. They divide my garments among them and* cast lots for my clothing (Ps. 22:14–18).

"He did not die for His own sins but for *our sins*:

> *. . . we considered him stricken by God, smitten by him, and afflicted. But he was pierced for our transgressions, he was crushed for our iniquities; the punishment that brought us peace was upon him, and by his wounds we are healed* (Is. 53:4,5).

"Incidently, the prophets go on to say His ancestry would be from the line of David (2 Sam. 7:12, 13), the Gentiles would follow Him (Is. 11:10), and He would be born in Bethlehem of Judah (Mic. 5:2). Did you know his mother was living in the wrong place until shortly before his birth? Mary had to go to Bethlehem for a special census for tax purposes at the precise moment of his birth!"

"O.K. already, so why don't the rabbis see this," she asked?

"Well, they saw this suffering servant Messiah and called Him 'Messiah ben (son of) Joseph.' But then they found just as many predictions about the Messiah reigning as King and ushering in an age of peace. They called Him 'Messiah ben David,' like King David. How did they reconcile these supposedly contradictory roles? Their theory was that there were two distinct Messiahs. But today it is clear that it is one Messiah with two appearances. First, he came to initiate the New Covenant prophesied by Jeremiah, to change us from the inside out.

> *"The time is coming," declares the* Lord, *"when I will make a*

> *new covenant with the house of Israel . . . and will remember their sins no more"* (Jer. 31:31, 34).

"Since we humans are so unclean compared to the holiness of God, we always needed a mediator and the blood of an innocent animal to atone for our sins. During Temple days our intermediary was a high priest. Today, our intermediary cleanses us from all sins, the Lamb of God who takes away the sins of the whole world. Then, when we are clean, He actually takes up residence inside our body, which becomes His temple.

"Speaking of two appearances of the Messiah, did you know the first time Moses identified himself as our deliverer we rejected him? (Ex. 2:11–14). And the first time Joseph identified himself as our deliverer, his own brothers wanted to kill him (Gen. 37:8, 19). Jesus fits this same pattern. His second appearance will be when He comes to rule the world and to usher in an age of peace.

> *They will neither harm nor destroy on all my holy mountain, for the earth will be full of the knowledge of the* L*ORD as the waters cover the sea* (Is. 11:9).

"Today the rabbis teach us about His second coming, but never mention Messiah ben Joseph. I found out why when I participated in a debate with a rabbi at the University of Maryland. After the debate, I engaged a young orthodox rabbinical student in dialogue. I asked him to tell me who Isaiah was speaking of in the fifty-third chapter. He amazed me with his answer. He said, 'I can't tell you.'

"'Why?,' I quickly asked. 'You know Hebrew better than I. Read it from your Tanakh (Old Covenant).' "

" 'No,' he responded, 'it would be a sin.' "

" 'Why?,' I asked again."

" 'Because I am not holy enough,' he said. 'We can only tell you what the rabbis who lived closer to the days of Moses tell us the verse means.' "

"How sad, Mom. What he was really saying was he *could not think for himself*."

Although I thought my presentation to my mother was overwhelming, she let me know she was grateful for the change believing in Jesus had caused in my life, but was not ready to accept the truth. "What would your father say? Are you hungry? Can I get you something to eat?"

Chapter Nineteen

"I Believe"

One day I saw my mother walking up my driveway with what I affectionately called care packages. She loved to bring my sister and me groceries. As I watched, she fell down. I rushed out immediately to help her. My mother was a heavy woman and I could see she had done considerable damage to her knee. It was puffed up and began to turn all the colors of the rainbow. I was worried. I said, "Mom, can I pray for you?" When she agreed, I said under my breath, "Lord if you ever answered a prayer, now is the time." And before my eyes and my mother's eyes, the swelling went down and the discoloration virtually disappeared.

After that healing, whenever my mother was sick, she would call me and expect God to heal her through my prayers. And she started adding a new phrase to her vocabulary. She would often express aloud the words, "Praise the Lord."

Then one day my aunt, who had diabetes, developed gangrene of the big toe. Her Jewish doctor said the only way to save her foot was to amputate her toe right away. With that, my mother boldly asked the doctor, "Could we wait a day so my son could pray for her?"

"Lady," he replied, "not even Jesus Christ could save that toe."

Before God, the devil, the angels in heaven, my mother and the Jewish doctor, I proclaim to you my aunt's toe was never amputated.

And one day my mother said to me, "Sidney, I no longer believe in Jesus because of *your* faith. I believe in Jesus as my Messiah because *I* believe."

■

I had just returned from a trip to Israel and called home to ask my wife to pick me up from the airport. When my daughter Leigh answered the phone, she was crying.

I said, "What's wrong?"

"Something horrible happened," she said. "Grandma is dead."

Composing myself quickly, I tried to calm Leigh, by saying, "Grandma is in heaven."

"I know Dad, but I'm going to miss her."

Chapter Twenty

Who Is a True Jew?

After my mother's funeral, my father had only one question: Was I going to say the prayers (Kaddish) for my mother in the synagogue every day for eleven months? There was an ulterior motive behind my father's question. If I would say the prayers for my mother, he could be assured that I would say them for him. And it was his belief that somehow these prayers would be his ticket into heaven without punishment or delay. Since he knew I did not agree with this form of prayer, he wondered what my answer would be. For a split second I thought of the time commitment. I thought of the endurance needed to sit through all the rituals and prayers in a language I did not understand. I thought of the possible repercussions by those in the synagogue who knew of my outspoken faith in Jesus. But as quickly as these thoughts raced through my mind, I found myself agreeing to do it.

It had been years since I had put on the tefillin (little box with Scripture inside that is wrapped around one's head and arm to conform to Deut. 6:8). A retired rabbi helped me as I placed the tefillin around my arm and on my head. There was a good feeling in worshipping with my people and participating in rituals that have been observed for thousands of years.

After one service, I got into a conversation with the man who read from the Torah. The Torah reading happened to be about the Jewish people walking through the Red Sea as though it were dry land. As I discussed this with my friend, he looked at me with the most incredulous expression and said, "You don't really believe those stories, do you?"

I responded with just as incredulous an expression and said, "You don't? What are you doing here?"

It is one thing when a secular Jew does not believe in the Torah. But when a Jewish religious leader does not believe in the Torah, it shocks me. Then, when he told me he did not believe in God or life after death, I really was curious why he was even attending the synagogue. He responded, "Because my friends are here. Because I like the traditions of my fathers. And because it gives me something to do." I always thought these elderly men who davined (prayed) every day at the minyan (a gathering of ten or more Jewish men to pray) were the most holy Jews in the synagogue. I found that many of the men I prayed with felt the same way as this man.

My father greatly appreciated my going to the synagogue every day to pray. And since I had not mentioned Jesus in a while, he asked, "Do you still believe in Him?" I had been waiting for God's timing because every time I mentioned Jesus, my father would always get angry. I told him that I believed in Jesus and He was the reason I was going to the synagogue. I told him I did not believe the prayers were necessary for Mom because she was already in heaven. At that, he got angry and I quickly changed the subject.

On another occasion my father said men from the synagogue had told him that their sons would not have been so faithful to go to the synagogue every day. My father would say to me, "You're a wonderful son. You're as good as gold. But do you have to believe in *Him*?"

The Talmud declares that if a voice from heaven should contradict the majority of rabbis, we must ignore that voice. A *true* Jew says that if the Torah contradicts the majority of rabbis, we must follow the Torah.

May God grant that soon all Israel would be *true* Jews.

Chapter Twenty-One

Heaven Must Be A Wonderful Place

You would have to be Jewish to understand my father's attitude about Yeshua. Born in Poland and raised in an orthodox Jewish home, when his father passed by a church, he spit at it. Christians, his father would say, were responsible for killing more Jews than any other group of people.

For years I tried to convince my father that not everyone who called himself a Christian was a true follower of Jesus. A true Christian has experienced a spiritual rebirth and could be identified by his unconditional love. But my father never appeared to understand nor did he seem to have even a slight interest in Jesus.

I had a holy mandate to win my father to the Lord. And even though I had no evidence in the natural, I knew one day he would become a Messianic Jew. But after twenty years of faith and confession and patience, every once in a while doubt would rear its ugly head and I would have to rebuke it.

Sunday evening, November 1, 1992, I got a call from my sister, from the intensive care unit of a hospital in the Washington, D.C. area. She told me that Dad was bleeding and that the doctors didn't know why. She said that he might be dead within a few hours. If he survived, he would only live a few days.

Because I lived in another part of the country, I had to trust God that Dad would survive the night. I flew to Washington, D.C. the following morning. My dad had come close to death before, but I was completely certain that he would not die until he received the Messiah.

On Monday, when I arrived, I immediately went to his bed. I began telling my father that it was necessary for him to have his sins forgiven in order to be with my mother in heaven. Every time I had promised my mother that Dad would become a believer, she sadly shook her head. She didn't have the faith to believe for such a miracle, she would tell me. But he knew that she had believed. She had told him many times, "Heaven must be a wonderful place."

That Monday in the hospital, my father was so weak that he could only grunt in response to my questions. When my sister and I asked him if he believed Jesus was his Messiah, he answered, but neither of us could understand what he said.

The next day we asked him once again. This time he clearly and loudly said a resounding, "Yes." My sister leaped for joy right there in intensive care. Someone later said he had only done it to please us. But on his death bed the last thing an orthodox Jew would do is confess Jesus as Lord unless he meant it.

The next morning, when I saw my father, I knew he was slipping away. He looked into my eyes. Then I heard the nurse say he was gone.

Shalom, Dad. Good-bye. *Le hitra ot.* I'll see you again.

Chapter Twenty-Two

There Must Be Something More!

Many years ago, I wrote a song called, "There Must Be Something More!" It was more than a song. It was a cry of my heart for reality and meaning and purpose to life.

God has abundantly answered that cry. Joy and I just celebrated our thirtieth wedding anniversary. And I can honestly say that Joy is the joy of my life. Our daughter Leigh graduated from Oral Roberts University and is now married to Greg Williamson. Both of them have a strong faith in the Messiah. If I had searched throughout the whole world, I could not have found a better husband for my daughter. And they presented us with our first grandchild, Olivia.

I have personally seen the power of God heal the crippled, open deaf ears, and cause the blind to see. Cancers and tumors have been removed and people imprisoned from fears, depression, and bondages have been set free. There is more power in one word from God than all the power of the new age combined.

In 1977, I started the Messianic Vision. Through mass media, I am dedicated to making the love of God known to all people.

For me, my life nearly ended in insanity, a wrecked marriage, even suicide. I am one grateful Jewish man who found there *is* something more.

Chapter Twenty-Three

Your Search

The following articles will give you key information to consider in your search for something more. May God give you understanding of His truth…

THE BIBLE IS TRUE

These Scriptures will help you to establish the truth of God's Word. All prophecies are from the Jewish Scriptures.

PRESERVATION OF THE JEWISH PEOPLE

This is what the LORD *says, he who appoints the sun to shine by day, who decrees the moon and stars to shine by night, who stirs up the sea so that its waves roar—the* LORD *Almighty is his name: "Only if these decrees vanish from my sight" declares the* LORD, *"will the descendants of Israel ever cease to be a nation before me"* (Jer. 31:35, 36).

DISPERSION OF THE JEWISH PEOPLE

You who were as numerous as the stars in the sky will be left but few in number, because you did not obey the LORD *your God . . . . Then the* LORD *will scatter you among all nations, from one end of the earth to the other. There you will worship other gods—gods of wood and stone, which neither you nor your fathers have known* (Deut. 28:62, 64).

SURVIVAL OF THE JEWISH PEOPLE

Yet in spite of this, when they are in the land of their enemies,

> *I will not reject them or abhor them so as to destroy them completely, breaking my covenant with them. I am the LORD their God* (Lev. 26:44).

FORMATION OF ISRAEL AND REGATHERING OF THE JEWISH PEOPLE

> *In that day the LORD will reach out his hand a second time to reclaim the remnant that is left of his people .... He will raise a banner for the nations and gather the exiles of Israel; he will assemble the scattered people of Judah from the four quarters of the earth* (Is. 11:11, 12).

ISRAEL REBUILT

> *They will rebuild the ruined cities and live in them ...* (Amos 9:14).

AGRICULTURAL ACHIEVEMENTS

> *The desert and the parched land will be glad; the wilderness will rejoice and blossom* (Is. 35:1).

JERUSALEM: A BURDEN FOR ALL PEOPLE

> *I am going to make Jerusalem a cup that sends all the surrounding peoples reeling. Judah will be besieged as well as Jerusalem. On that day, when all the nations of the earth are gathered against her, I will make Jerusalem an immovable rock for all the nations. All who try to move it will injure themselves* (Zech. 12:2, 3).

ALL NATIONS WILL TURN AGAINST ISRAEL

> *I will gather all the nations to Jerusalem to fight against it ...*" (Zech. 14:2).

> *"In the whole land," declares the LORD, "two-thirds will be struck down and perish ..."* (Zech. 13:8).

SHALOM WITH GOD

Do the Jewish Scriptures talk about life after death? Daniel says:

> *Multitudes who sleep in the dust of the earth will awake: some to everlasting life, others to shame and everlasting contempt* (Dan. 12:2).

How can we awake to everlasting life? By not being separated from God. The Bible says all of us are separated from God. We read in Psalm 14:3:

> *All have turned aside, they have together become corrupt; there is no one who does good, not even one.*

And in Isaiah 59:2:

> *But your iniquities have separated you from your God . . . .*

God gave us a way of "covering our sins" (atonement) through the sacrifice of an unblemished animal in the Temple:

> *It is the blood that makes atonement for one's life* (Lev. 17:11).

Since the Temple was destroyed in A.D. 70, animal sacrifices for atonement are impossible. How can we have the blood of atonement today?

Jeremiah predicted a New Covenant for the house of Israel and Judah:

> *"The time is coming," declares the* Lord, *"when I will make a new covenant with the house of Israel.... and will remember their sins no more"* (Jer. 31:31, 34).

God provided this New Covenant blood of atonement through a perfect sacrificial Lamb, one called "The Messiah." Isaiah described how to recognize Him:

> *Who has believed our message and to whom has the arm of the* Lord *been revealed?... He had no beauty or majesty to attract us to him, nothing in his appearance that we should desire him. He was despised and rejected by men, a man of sorrows, and familiar with suffering. Like one from whom men hide their faces he was despised, and we esteemed him not. Surely he took up our infirmities and carried our sorrows, yet we considered him stricken by God, smitten by him, and afflicted. But he was pierced for our transgressions, he was crushed for our iniquities; the punishment that brought us peace was upon him, and by his wounds we are healed. We all, like sheep, have gone astray, each of us has turned to his own way; and the* Lord *has laid on him the iniquity of us all* (Is. 53:1–6).

God made sure we could recognize the Messiah by giving us over 300 identifying marks as described by the prophets of Israel.

HE WOULD BE BORN IN BETHLEHEM OF JUDAH

But you, Bethlehem Ephrathah, though you are small among the clans of Judah, out of you will come for me one who will be ruler over Israel, whose origins are from of old, from ancient times (Mic. 5:2).

HIS ANCESTRY WAS TO BE OF THE FAMILY OF DAVID

"The days are coming," declares the LORD, "when I will raise up to David a righteous Branch . . . . This is the name by which he will be called: The LORD Our Righteousness" (Jer. 23:5,6).

THE GENTILES WILL FOLLOW HIM

In that day the Root of Jesse will stand as a banner for the peoples; the nations will rally to him, and his place of rest will be glorious (Is. 11:10).

HE WAS TO DIE *BEFORE* THE SECOND TEMPLE WAS DESTROYED

After the sixty-two "sevens," the Anointed One will be cut off and will have nothing. The people of the ruler who will come will destroy the city [Jerusalem] *and the sanctuary* (Dan. 9:26). [The Temple was destroyed in A.D. 70.]

Since God has provided the blood of Atonement through Messiah Yeshua (Jesus), we must repent (admit we have sinned and turn from unrighteousness) and ask for forgiveness in the name of Yeshua. Each individual's prayer should be:

> "Messiah Yeshua, I admit that I have sinned. I believe that You have provided the blood of atonement for me. I receive You now as my Messiah and Lord. Thank You for giving me *shalom* with God."

DIALOGUE

■ *I was born a Jew and I will die a Jew!*

You do not give up your Jewish identity to receive Jesus. On the contrary, you gain a personal relationship with the God of Abraham, Isaac and Jacob through your walk with the Jewish Messiah.

■ *A person is either Jewish or Christian. I'm Jewish.*

No, you are either Jewish, Gentile or of the Messiah. Non-Jewish (Gentile) followers of Messiah Jesus are called Christians; many Jewish believers in the Messiah prefer to be called Messianic Jews.

■ *Doesn't belief in Jesus mean that you're no longer Jewish?*

This question really isn't the issue. The question "How can you be Jewish and believe in Jesus?" is better answered with another question: "Who is Jesus?"

If Jesus, as claimed, is Israel's promised Messiah, then, according to the Scriptures, in order to be a truly observant Jew, one must acknowledge and believe in Jesus as the Messiah.

One is either Jewish or Gentile by birth—nothing can change that. According to the Bible, a Jew is a person who is descended from Abraham, Isaac and Jacob.

Jesus and His earliest followers were Jewish. They never renounced their Jewish heritage. Nor were they expected to do so. Believing in—and trusting—the Jewish Messiah can add to one's appreciation of Judaism.

■ *If Jesus is the Jewish Messiah, why don't more Jews believe in Him?*

Judaism today is divided into various groups: Reformed, Reconstructionist, Conservative, Orthodox, and Hasidic. Each group accepts certain truths from the Talmud and certain truths from the Bible. The distinctive quality of Messianic Judaism is that it is biblically Jewish, i.e., it holds to the absolute authority of the Scriptures. This is important because to all other Jewish groups, the *Bible is not the final authority.* Therefore, the Messiahship of Jesus is *not* an issue that is approached with an open mind, since the interpretations of today's rabbis depend totally on the opinions and traditions of their forefathers who rejected Jesus.

Those Jews who *have* studied the question of the Messianic claims of Jesus with a truly open mind have come to surprising conclusions, and many rabbis and Jewish leaders have indeed accepted Jesus as their Messiah. Some Jewish people have rejected Jesus because they fail to understand His dual role. They have looked for a king, a political leader who would free them from their oppressors and provide peace and prosperity. Jesus will accomplish this in the future, when He returns to re-establish the throne of David.

The Hebrew Scriptures indicate that the Jewish people would not recognize their Messiah when He first appeared (Is. 53:1–3) to die as an atonement for sin.

■ *We Jews believe in one God, not three.*

Followers of Jesus also believe in one God, not three. Most

Jews recite the Shema, the Jewish confession of faith, "Hear O Israel, the LORD our God, *the Lord is one*." However, the translation of the New Jewish Version, recognized as the most accurate English translation produced by Jewish scholars, states: "Hear O Israel, the LORD is our God, *the LORD alone*." The point of the Shema is to demand absolute faith in the LORD alone, with no gods before Him. The Hebrew word "*echad*," translated "alone" here, means "one" in the sense of "that one alone."

In the twelfth century, Moses Maimonides, writing to counter Christian and Muslim beliefs, compiled his thirteen articles of faith, recited by observant Jews daily. One of the articles states that Jews must believe that God is *yachid*—"absolute unity." But this is unscriptural, since the Hebrew Bible gives clear indications of God's composite unity.

Genesis 19:24 states that "the LORD rained down burning sulfur on Sodom and Gomorrah, from the LORD out of the heavens." In other words, the LORD, *who had been on the earth talking to Abraham* (read Gen. 18:1–33 very carefully), rained down fire and brimstone from the LORD *out of the heavens.*

The Spirit of God came upon many people in the Scriptures. For instance, Isaiah 61:1 states, "The Spirit of the Sovereign LORD is on me . . . ."

And, finally, who is God's *Son* in Proverbs 30:4?

> *Who has gone up to heaven and come down? Who has gathered up the wind in the hollow of his hands? Who has wrapped up the waters in his cloak? Who has established all the ends of the earth? What is his name, and the name of his son? Tell me if you know!*

Isaiah 42:1 speaks of God's servant (that is, the Messiah) upon whom God places His Spirit so that "he will bring justice to the nations." Here in one passage is a reference to the LORD (the Father), the Messiah (the Son), and the Spirit.

> *Here is my servant, whom I uphold, my chosen one in whom I delight; I will put my Spirit on him and he will bring justice to the nations.*

■ *Jewish people don't need a middleman.*

Judaism historically has required a priesthood, the Levites, to minister between the Israelites and their holy God. Leviticus 1:15 directed that only a priest (one of Aaron's sons) could sprinkle the blood of atonement in the Tent of Meeting for the forgiveness of sin.

Followers of Jesus now have direct access to God through the mediatorial role performed by Jesus. We now approach the LORD directly and go right into His holy presence. No Jew in Bible days, aside from the High Priest (and at that, only once a year), could ever do this.

■ *Jewish people do not believe in human sacrifice.*

Followers of Jesus do not believe in this either. We as human beings have no right to sacrifice another human being for our sins. Only God has the absolute right to give life and take it away. Because the penalty for sin is death (Ezek. 18:4), God, in His great mercy, provided His own sacrifice to pay for the sins of the world. His own Son willingly suffered the death penalty for us.

It is the absolutely clear teaching of Isaiah 53 that God would place the punishment due His people upon an innocent and righteous sufferer who would die for Israel's sins. This prophecy was fulfilled by Jesus the Messiah.

■ *Judaism does not believe in original sin.*

Depending on one's definition of original sin, one may say that Judaism does or does not believe in this teaching. Psalm 51:5, which states, "Surely I was sinful at birth, sinful from the time my mother conceived me," clearly teaches the inherent sinfulness of man. And, according to some Jewish traditions, all human souls were in Adam when he sinned. Thus, when Adam sinned, the entire human race fell with him.

There can be no question, however, that the Hebrew Bible teaches the *universality* of sin. Genesis 8:21 says that "every inclination [Hebrew, *yetzer*] of [man's] heart is evil from childhood." And Ecclesiastes 7:20 says, "There is not a righteous man on earth who does what is right and never sins." Proverbs 20:9 asks, "Who can say, 'I have kept my heart pure; I am clean and without sin?'" And Isaiah 53:6 states that "We all, like sheep, have gone astray, each of us has turned to his own way." The sinfulness of man is clearly taught throughout the entire Hebrew Bible.

■ *Religions are all alike. They all have some good points and can help people to lead worthwhile lives.*

Faith in the Messiah is not a religion; it is God's declared way for mankind to be reconciled to Him. While there are many good points to commend in some religions, this does not mean that God is satisfied with everything in "religion."

What is important is not what man decides about God, but rather what God decides about man. We must approach God according to *His* standards. It is not up to us to devise our own way of approaching Him. Since He has given us a way to have our sins forgiven, then it is our *privilege* to accept His grace.

■ *Why did God allow six million Jews to die in the Holocaust?*

> *The secret things belong to the* L*ORD* *our God, but the things revealed belong to us . . .* (Deut. 29:29).

God has chosen to keep some of the reasons for the holocaust a mystery. But some reasons have been revealed.

God tells us that if we obeyed the law, we would be a nation of priests and blessed above all people on the face of the earth. However, if we violated the law, we would lose our homeland and be scattered to the four corners of the earth. And wherever we would go, we would be persecuted (Deut. 28).

It was as if God's law were a picket fence of protection around us. However, once we went out of the gate of protection, we would be destroyed!

In addition to this warning in His Word, God always sent prophets calling for repentance in the hope judgment could be averted. Sometimes we repented as the Ninevites did when warned by Jonah, and sometimes we ignored God's message, as in Jerusalem when Jeremiah warned of Nebuchadnezzar's invasion. Before the holocaust of Hitler, God warned us through fiery Zionists like Theodor Herzl and Ze'ev Jabotinsky. In 1939, Jabotinsky said, "I see a horrible vision. Time is growing short for you to be spared."

Even with the warnings, why a God of love allowed the holocaust is a secret we will not fully understand until we get to heaven.

■ *What happens to Jews who do not believe in Jesus?*

The only way to be granted forgiveness of sin is belief in Jesus. Jesus said, "Hear, O Israel, the Lord our God, the Lord is one" (Mark 12:29). This is called the Shema and is chanted by God-fearing Jews.

Jeremiah (29:13) says, "You will seek me and find me when you seek me with all your heart."

Some believe that many Jews, sincerely seeking God, died with the Shema on their lips and had revelations of Jesus in concentration camps and during other times of trial and tribulation.

Only God knows those who are seeking Him with all their heart. We cannot know what is in any heart but our own. Who do *you* say Jesus is?

■ *How can a virgin have a child?*

Is anything impossible for God? Sarah gave birth to Isaac when she was past ninety. Besides, which is more difficult: for a virgin to conceive, or for God to create a human being from dust?

Actually, Messianic prophecy indicates that while Messiah was to be a real man, He was also to be greater than any man, one of His titles even being "Mighty God" (Is. 9:6; 9:5 in some versions). The virgin birth explains how this could be possible: Messiah would be born by human *and* divine means.

The Hebrew word in Isaiah 7:14 can *today* be translated "virgin" or "a young unmarried woman." Interestingly enough, when Jewish scholars translated Isaiah 7:14 into Greek (Septuagint) about two hundred years *before* Jesus, they translated the Hebrew word *'almah* with the Greek word *parthenos* which means "virgin." It is this Jewish translation which Matthew quoted in Matthew 1:23.

It is clear that the Messiah, who was to be a special and supernatural person, had a special and supernatural birth.

■ *Christians have always hated and persecuted the Jewish people.*

Not everyone who calls himself a Christian *is* a Christian. Jesus, who commanded His followers to love all men, said:

> *Watch out for false prophets. They come to you in sheep's clothing, but inwardly they are ferocious wolves. By their fruit you will recognize them* (Matt. 7:15–16).

If a person does not bear the Christian "fruit" of love, compassion and mercy, then he has no right to call himself a Christian.

■ *Do Jewish people need to repent?*

The Hebrew word for "repent" is *shuv* (pronounced *shoov*), and it literally means, "turn, turn back." Many times God spoke through His prophets to Israel saying: "Turn back to Me and I will turn back to you" (see, e.g., Zech. 1:3–4; Joel 2:12–14). In other words, if Israel would *repent*, then God would *relent*.

But do Jews need to "turn back" today? The answer is emphatically "Yes!" since: 1) all Jews are members of the human race; 2) all human beings sin; 3) whoever sins "turns away" from God; and 4) whoever has "turned away" needs to "turn back"!

Have you sinned in thought, word, or deed? Have you stolen something, or committed a lustful act, or hated someone in your heart, or been ungrateful, or abused your body, or told a lie, or been filled with pride? Is there any way at all, be it large or small, that you have turned away from God? Then whoever you are, Jew or Gentile, you need to repent ("turn back")!

■ *Doesn't Isaiah 53 refer to the Jewish people as a whole?*

The earliest Jewish interpretations of chapter 53, which really begins with Isaiah 52:13, said that it spoke of the Messiah. It is clear for many reasons that it *cannot* refer to the Jewish people as a whole, or even to a righteous remnant within the nation. This passage also *cannot* refer to the "Messianic Age" because verse three would then have the people reject a utopia: "He was despised and rejected by men, a man of sorrows . . ." (Is. 53:3). Furthermore, Israel has never been a silent sufferer: ". . . so he did not open his mouth" (Is. 53:7b). And, who is "my people" if "he" refers to Israel? ". . . For he was cut off from the land of the living; for the transgression of my people he was stricken" (Is. 53:8b).

The prophet Hosea describes Israel as a harlot; Israel, unlike the Messiah described in the passage, is *not* without sin: ". . . nor was any deceit in his mouth" (Is. 53:9b).

Furthermore, according to the Torah, the Jewish people would only suffer if they were *un*righteous. Nowhere is it ever taught that Israel would suffer for the sins of the world. Only Jesus has ever fulfilled this prophecy.

WHO IS HE?
BY DR. MICHAEL BROWN

Jesus—Yeshua.
Rabbi? Prophet? Healer? Deliverer?
Savior?
Messiah?
Son of God?
Jesus—Yeshua.
Deceiver? Apostate? Magician?
Rebel? Traitor? Liar?
Accursed of God?
Jesus—Yeshua. Who is He?

Two thousand years have come and gone, but the question remains the same: Is Jesus of Nazareth the Jewish Messiah, the Savior of the world? If He is, then let's follow Him, for we have no other way. If He's not, let's expose Him, for only the truth will set us free.

Although the world is full of religions, the controversy surrounding the Messiahship of Jesus is unique, because both those who accept Jesus and those who reject Him base their beliefs on one and the same book. Jews who follow Jesus say: "He must be the Messiah. He fulfilled *all* the prophecies of the Bible." Jews who don't follow Jesus say: "He can't be the Messiah. He fulfilled *none* of the prophecies of the Bible."

Who's right?

From one book, the Hebrew Scriptures, have come two faiths. One faith says: We'd rather die than *confess* the name of Jesus. The other faith says: We'd rather die than *deny* the name of Jesus. One faith says: There are two Messiahs who will come only once.[3] The other faith says: There is one Messiah but He will come twice.

So how can *I* know the truth?

Simple. Only one of these two faiths has really followed the Bible. The other has gone its own way. Only one has really continued in the power of God. The other has followed the traditions of men. If we listen carefully to the voice of God, then His Word will be "a light to our path and a lamp to our feet." His Word is sure. He cannot lie.

Recently I was speaking to a well educated ultra-orthodox rabbi about the Messiahship of Jesus. He didn't want to hear my opinions (and I can't blame him for that!). He didn't care about what anybody else had to say. He just wanted to go back to the original sources. "Let's go back to the Talmud," he said. "That's where we can find the truth."

I think my answer surprised him. "Why should I go back to the Talmud," I said, "when I can go all the way back to the New Testament?" To *my* surprise, he didn't argue.

You see, many Jewish people today are told that Judaism alone is the real religion of the Bible, and that "Christianity" is a much

---

[3]Although most traditional Jews are unaware of the teaching of the two Messiahs, one who will suffer and die in the last great war, and one who will rule and reign, this is the teaching of the Talmud and most of the early Jewish writings. For a clear statement, see the Babylonian Talmud, Sukkah 52a.

later, predominantly Gentile religion. And yet statements such as these, intimidating as they may sound, are simply not true.

Here are the facts: traditional Judaism as we know it today is absolutely *not* the religion of Moses and the prophets. It is the religion of the rabbis who lived and taught over 1500 years later. Instead of being the religion of Temple and sacrifice as prescribed by the Torah, it is the religion of *no* Temple and *no* sacrifice, in spite of the Torah. It may shock you to know this, but some of Judaism's most sacred books did not even *exist* before the late Middle Ages. Christopher Columbus had already discovered America before the Code of the Jewish Law used by orthodox Jews today had ever been compiled!

As for Messianic Judaism, the Judaism that believes in Yeshua the Messiah, the facts are as follows: the sole authority for faith and practice is the Bible, consisting of the Old and New Covenants. Rather than the New Covenant being a late Gentile book, all its authors, except one, were Jews, Jews who lived in the days *before* the second Temple was destroyed in 70 C.E. Many other traditions and customs added in the following centuries by the church have had nothing to do with the Bible and therefore have absolutely no connection with Messianic Judaism. Although some people may call them "biblical" or "Christian," they are totally devoid of scriptural authority.

The writers of the New Covenant were Jews who recognized that Messiah had come to atone for the sins of His people. They based their beliefs on the Hebrew Scriptures, and on the Hebrew Scriptures alone. Thus they knew that Yeshua was the Jewish Messiah because He fulfilled the Old Covenant prophecies. *If He had not fulfilled the prophecies then they would not have followed Him.* They recognized Him because He fit the description perfectly.

Then why didn't the other Jewish leaders of the day acknowledge that Yeshua was in fact the Messiah? The answer again is simple: They weren't looking for Him. They were looking for another. The Messiah of the rabbis was not the Messiah of the Bible. And yet the thing they longed for most was the very thing they missed, *for Messiah had to come to save them from their sins.*

So in 30 C.E., as Yeshua "approached Jerusalem and saw the city, He wept over it and said, 'If you, even you, had only known on this day what would bring you peace—but now it is hidden from your eyes. For you did not recognize the time of God's coming to you.'" Forty years later Jerusalem was destroyed, and tens of thousands of her inhabitants were dead.

"But wait one second," you say. "Weren't these rabbis the very ones who studied the Law day and night? And weren't these the men who were responsible for some of the most beautiful prayers and teachings that were ever written? How did it happen, then, that some of the most scrupulous and zealous Jews who ever lived missed the Messiah?" It is to this question that we now must turn.

SUBSTITUTION.

There is no more important word in the Hebrew Bible than this if we are to understand God's holy love for us—substitution.

It is the key that unlocks the door to our redemption. And it is the rock that makes men stumble. *It alone can fully explain why Yeshua's own people missed Him, and it alone can open their eyes again.* Substitution. Without this word Yeshua's death is a farce.

The rabbis of the Talmud debated about how to be made right with God. While some recognized that "there is no atonement without the blood," they didn't all agree on the rest. Some said, "For certain sins, the Day of Atonement alone is sufficient." Others argued, "No! There must be repentance as well." Some claimed that only the Day, *plus* repentance, *plus* suffering would do the trick, while there were those who said, "The only hope for forgiveness is in the Day of Atonement and death!"

And yet they missed the point of the Day, missed the point of the blood. They failed to grasp the lesson that was before their eyes.

Day after day, the Sadducees offered their sacrifices at the Temple. Thousands upon thousands of animals were slain, and gallons of blood were poured out on the altar. Lambs and goats and rams and calves were offered up to a holy God. Yet the people could not see.

The Pharisees studied the Torah day and night. They added new regulations to old laws, and they developed the most detailed system of ritual purity that the world has ever known. They taught that *study* of the Law was more loved by God than even the offerings themselves. Yet they failed to see the heart of the matter. They failed to grasp the fundamental meaning of it all.

For it was not the blood of bulls that God wanted for Himself; it was not the fat of rams that He desired. It was not a people of outward holiness that He sought; He did not require a new code that would keep men clean. No. He wanted a substitute, a righteous lamb who would bear His people's sins. He wanted a spotless sacrifice who would purify the people within.

Over and over again, a thousand times ten thousand, the offerings were brought before the altar. And over and over again, in numbers too great to count, their innocent blood was spilled. And over and over again, the message of God was crying out: "A substitute must come! A substitute must come!"

The Jewish people of Yeshua's day were all looking for a Savior. Some hoped for a mighty military leader, while others looked for a deliverer from the sky. Some looked for a holy priest, while others looked for a teacher of righteousness. Yet no one was looking for a crucified Messiah. And no one was looking for the Lamb of God. They had forgotten that the righteous Servant of the LORD was *Himself* to be an *'asham*—an offering for sin (Is. 53:10). And they had forgotten father Abraham's words that *God* would provide the lamb for the burnt offering (Gen. 22:8).

Yes, there *were* some rabbis who claimed that *every* sacrifice was accepted on the basis of Abraham's offering up of Isaac. And they claimed that in the Passover rite, when God "saw the blood" (Ex. 12), He was looking at the sacrifice of Isaac and *not* at the blood of the lamb.

Yet Isaac was *not* offered, and his blood was never shed. And it was *God Himself* who provided the sacrifice that saved the life of Abraham's son.

It was *Messiah* who suffered and died, and it is by *His* wounds that we are healed (Is. 53:5). It was He who was led as a lamb to the slaughter, and it was He who bore our sins (Is. 53:7, 12 and Lev. 16:22).

Oh yes, there were Jewish teachers who believed that the suffering of the righteous could bring atonement to the world. Yet when the truly Righteous One suffered and died, they said that it was for nought.

Our rabbis tell us that when Messiah comes, He will establish peace on earth. When the real Savior comes, He will remove us from sin. *But a savior who takes us out of sin without taking the sin out of us is really no savior at all. And a Messiah who establishes peace on earth without first establishing peace in our hearts is really no Messiah at all.*

Messiah *had* to die. Messiah *had* to take our place. *There was no other way.* No other substitute was found. No one else could pay the price. Nothing else could heal our wounds, for sin required death.

Yeshua paid the price. It was *His* death that brought us life. *He* alone was the substitute for the sinful human race, and *He* alone can offer us redemption.

The traditional Judaism of our day has its roots in the religion of the Pharisees, a small group of Jews who banded together over two thousand years ago. These were the men who would not eat with ceremonially unwashed hands, the men so famous for their attention to detail. These were the men who even tithed on insignificant crops and who studied every jot and tittle of God's Law.

Yet many of these men missed Yeshua when He came. They did not see the forest for the trees.

For it is not ritual observance that makes a man clean within, and it is not attention to an outer system of laws that brings us to God. The heart of the Torah is to "love God with all our hearts, and to love our neighbor as ourselves." Yet this is the truth that these zealous men missed, since in their passion for the letter of the law they missed the spirit of the One who gave it.

And as the Pharisees went, so have the Jewish people gone.

Traditional Judaism as we know it today is the religion of those who rejected Yeshua. It is a decided reaction *against* faith in Him. It is a system which has been reconstructed to negate and counteract Messiah's real claims. That's why traditional Jews throughout the ages have stumbled over the person of Yeshua. But in the beginning it was not so.

The Jewish teachers *before* Yeshua emphasized the miraculous and believed in the power of God's testimony from heaven. But when the followers of Yeshua had all the healing cures, they said, "We don't depend on a miracle!"

Many of the Jews of Yeshua's day were looking for a deliverer who would come in the clouds of heaven. Yet when Yeshua came and said, "*I* will come again in the clouds of heaven," they said, "Not so! Our Messiah will be a teacher of the Law, a rabbi like ourselves!"

They had the prayers, they had the laws, they had the covenant tradition—how did our forefathers miss it? The answer again is simple. They truly had a zeal for God, but not according to knowledge (Rom. 10:2). They did not attain what they sought after, for they stumbled over the grace of God.

Messiah had come to make them well, yet they said in reply, "We're not sick!"

But not all of our forefathers missed it. The writer of almost half of the New Covenant was himself a Pharisee, born of the tribe of Benjamin. And the Book of Acts records "how many thousands of Jews" there were who believed and were zealous for the Torah (Acts 21:20). In fact, "a large number of [Jewish] priests became obedient to the faith" (Acts 6:7), and even today in our country and throughout the world, there are *tens of thousands* of Jews who believe and confess, "Yeshua is the Messiah! Yeshua is Lord!"

This, then, is the real Judaism, the Judaism that is truly Messianic. And this is the faith that will bring the world back to God, the faith that will cause the nations to believe. And Yeshua is the One who will establish justice in the earth, "and the coastlands shall [and do!] wait for His law!" (Is. 42:4, NKJV).

The Talmud teaches that for the last forty years before the Temple was destroyed, God did not accept the sacrifices of the Day of Atonement (Babylonian Talmud, Yoma 39). Year after year, for the life of one whole generation, the LORD was saying, "No."

You see, God had provided one sacrifice for all, a final atonement for the sins of mankind. God had provided the Lamb. And it was *forty years before the Temple was destroyed* that Yeshua offered His life. From that day to this, God has been saying "no" to His people. "No more of *your* sacrifices, no more of *your* prayers, no more of *your* works. I have provided the way."

Yet to all who have ears to hear, God has been saying: "Yes, you may come! Yes, you can know Me! Yes, I will cleanse you from *all* your sin! Believe in the One whom *I* have sent. Messiah Yeshua has come."

The spiritual leaders of our people who tell us that we cannot know God are wrong. They are only saying, "I don't know Him, so how can you? I've studied for years and I'm still learning. How can you be so sure?"

Once again, our answer is simple and clear. Messiah Yeshua has made God known. He has revealed the Father to us. And through His blood we have been brought back to God.

Tradition will not save us.
Opinions will not set us free.
Messiah has ransomed our souls from the pit.
Let all His Jewish people come!

ADVANCED DIALOGUE BY DR. MICHAEL BROWN

The New Covenant

■ *The New Covenant is anti-Semitic. It is filled with negative references to the Jewish people, and it blames them for the death of Yeshua.*

It is not difficult to show that the New Covenant is definitely *not* anti-Semitic. First, consider these facts:

1) All of the authors of the New Covenant, save one, were Jews. Their main topic was Yeshua, the Jewish Messiah, and much of their writing was addressed to a Jewish audience (e.g., the Gospel of Matthew or the Letter to the Hebrews).

2) The New Covenant has many positive things to say about the Jewish people. Yeshua himself taught that "salvation is from the Jews" (John 4:22b), and Paul (Saul) said that the Jewish people were "loved [by God] on account of the patriarchs" (i.e., Abraham, Isaac, and Jacob; Rom. 11:28b). In fact, Paul claimed that, from a spiritual standpoint, there was much advantage "in every way" in being born Jewish (Rom. 3:1–2), and that the Gentiles owed the Jewish people a material blessing, since they had partaken of the Jews' spiritual blessing (Rom. 15:27).

3) The heavenly city of Jerusalem, which is *the final destiny of all believers in Yeshua,* is said to have "a great, high wall with twelve gates" and the names written on these gates are "the names of the *twelve tribes of Israel*" (Rev. 21:12). In other words, *the only way into heaven is through Israel's gates.* This hardly sounds anti-Semitic!

What about the claim that the New Covenant also has many *negative* things to say about the Jewish people? Again, several answers can be given. First, the Hebrew prophets called their own people rebels, stiff-necked, and sinful, and they predicted that judgment would come upon them if they did not repent. This is exactly what God told His Jewish people. Were the Hebrew prophets anti-Semitic? Or is God anti-Semitic? Of course not! But these are the very things that the Jewish writers of the New Covenant said about *their own people*—that because they rejected the Messiah they were being just like their forefathers, stiff-necked and sinful, and that for this they would be judged. Does this make the New Covenant anti-Semitic?

Also, it is important to note that the term "Jews" in the New Covenant often refers to "Judaeans," or even "Judaean religious leaders." Thus, some of the negative comments spoken in the Gospel of John against "the Jews" are not meant to apply to *all* Jewish people, but rather to specific Jewish leaders in Judaea. For a clear example see John 9:22, where the *Jewish parents* of a blind man who had been miraculously healed were afraid of "*the Jews*" (i.e., some Pharisees; see 9:13–15, 40–41). Similarly, the Hebrew word *yehudi* (pronounced ye-hoo-*dee*) can either mean "Jew" or "Judaean." This explains a verse *in the Hebrew Scriptures* like Nehemiah 2:16, where Nehemiah, himself a Jew, refers to *another group* called "the Jews" (i.e., the inhabitants of Judaea), along with the priests, nobles, officials, "or any others who would be doing the work," all of whom were Jewish as well!

Finally, while some have claimed that Paul told his Gentile

readers (in this case the Thessalonians) that *the Jews* "displease God and are hostile to all men," it is important to read the overall context carefully (1 Thess. 2:14–16). When this is done, it will be seen at once that Paul is speaking about *those* Jews "who killed the Lord Jesus and the prophets," and now persecute us "in their effort to keep us from speaking to the Gentiles so that they may be saved." And this, says Paul, is exactly what the Thessalonians were suffering from *their* own countrymen (i.e., not *all* Thessalonians, but rather those who opposed the faith).

When all these facts are considered with an open mind, it is quite clear that the New Covenant is *not* an anti-Semitic work. Thus many scholars today emphasize that if you want to understand the New Covenant fully, you must read it as a thoroughly Jewish Book!

■ *The New Covenant is full of historical inaccuracies. It frequently misquotes and misunderstands the Hebrew Scriptures.*

As far as the historical accuracy of the New Covenant is concerned, it should be noted that of *every* book written in the ancient world, the Greek New Covenant is far and away the best preserved. There are literally *thousands* of ancient manuscripts containing copies of either part or all of the New Covenant books. And, in spite of the abundance of ancient manuscript evidence, these documents contain virtually *no disagreements* on any major doctrinal point.

As more and more research has been done into the customs and history of first-century Palestine and Asia Minor, the New Covenant has emerged as a prime historical source of great value, either confirming or supplementing what archaeology has taught us. Furthermore, studies by modern Jewish scholars have served to underscore the Jewishness of Jesus and the New Covenant authors.

The New Covenant's use of the Old Covenant has also been found to be thoroughly Jewish. Because the New Covenant was written in Greek while the Old Covenant was written in Hebrew, the writers often quoted from the Greek version of their day, the Septuagint. But this version was made by *Jews* some two hundred years *before* Yeshua was born. And, although on certain occasions the *wording* of an Old Covenant verse may seem to change when it is quoted in the New Covenant, this is often due to the fact that the *Jewish Septuagint* was being quoted! These "differences," then, do *not* reflect later, "Christian" changes; and, more importantly, the *actual meaning* of the verses *never* changes.

Another major factor to be considered is that the New Covenant writers, who, with the exception of one medical doctor, Luke, were all Jews, often followed the *Jewish interpretative rules* of the day. It was as Jews that they read their Scriptures, and it was as Jews that they interpreted their Scriptures! Thus, some of their quotations of the Hebrew Scriptures are in keeping with the *common Jewish understanding* of the passage that they were citing. At other times, the main difference in interpretation was due to the fact that they understood that the Messiah had *already* come, and, rather than waiting for a future fulfillment of the Scriptures, they saw them as already being fulfilled. And there are some New Covenant quotations that reflect the interpretation found in the Aramaic paraphrases (called Targums—"translations") which were then being read in the *synagogues.* Again, this means that the New Covenant writers were being thoroughly *Jewish* in their handling of the Hebrew text.

It is also important to remember that the Jews in the first century of this era were primarily concerned with determining what the Scriptures were saying to *them*, in *their* day and age. Their primary concern was not in rediscovering what Amos or Isaiah had said to *his* contemporaries. They wanted to know what God required of them in the present tense, and they wanted to know what He had promised them. Thus, the Jews who authored what we now call the Dead Sea Scrolls moved into an isolated life of study and discipline *based on their interpretation of the Hebrew Bible.* The Pharisees began to develop a detailed system of laws and regulations *based on their interpretation of the Hebrew Bible.* And the writers of the New Covenant received and followed Yeshua as Messiah *based on their interpretation of the Hebrew Bible.*

Of these three different systems of Jewish interpretation, that of the New Covenant most accurately adheres to the proper understanding of the Hebrew text. In fact, in comparison to the *Jewish* interpretation of Scripture as found in the Talmud and Midrash, the New Covenant writers were amazingly careful and sober.

Any time the New Covenant interpretation does seem hard to follow, one need only remember these three facts: (1) the writers may have been quoting the Septuagint, the *Jewish* Greek version of the day (the *wording* may be slightly different, but the *meaning* is the same); (2) they may have been following an unusual *Rabbinic* method of interpretation (while our twentieth-century Western minds may have a hard time following their line of reason, a first-century rabbi would have had no problem grasping their point); and (3) they were able to find hints and indicators of Messiah's life and ministry on virtually every page of the Hebrew Bible, since, along with many other first-century Jews, they rightly believed that all the Hebrew prophets and the entire history of ancient Israel pointed to the coming of the Messiah. Therefore, although they did not disregard the original contextual meaning of the passages which they quoted, their primary purpose was to show how wonderfully all Old Covenant history and revelation were brought to their fullness (i.e., were fulfilled) in Yeshua the Messiah.

Although many Jews of today claim that the New Covenant authors contradict themselves, not a single Jew in ancient times ever raised such an argument! If there were so many gross errors and mistakes, why didn't those who opposed the faith point these things out back then? The answer, of course, is that according to all standards of ancient history writing, the New Covenant documents were a first-rate piece of work. And if, as some claim, the Jews who wrote the New Covenant were cunning men who were willing to lie and deceive, then why didn't they make up a story that no one could argue with, not even their opponents? Obviously, they were just reporting the facts as they saw them, and none of their contemporaries could disagree!

One early follower of Yeshua pointed out that there is an amazing *overall harmony* that exists in the Gospel accounts of our Messiah. He stated that any *apparent* discrepancies which might be noticed could be explained only if we understood that each of the eyewitnesses was accurately reporting what he saw and heard. Thus, if we ourselves were there at the time the event occurred, we would see how perfectly all the pieces of the puzzle fit together to form one clear picture of the life and teaching of the Son of God. Therefore, rather than being evidence of poor memory and lies, the different perspectives of the various New Covenant authors help us realize just how accurate their accounts really were.

Some of the greatest minds this world has ever seen have devoted their entire lives to the careful study of the New Testament text, and some of history's greatest skeptics have attacked it. *There is nothing new that today's critics will discover.* The New Covenant has endured the test of time. It continues to be worthy of our faith.

■ *Yeshua didn't fulfill any of the Messianic prophecies. We know that the New Covenant writers actually reconstructed the life of Yeshua so as to harmonize it with certain predictions made by the prophets.*

These two statements are mutually contradictory. Why would the New Covenant writers *intentionally* rewrite the events of Yeshua's life so as to make Him fulfill predictions that were not really Messianic? If the prophecies that they quoted were really non-Messianic, then why did they "make" Yeshua's life conform to them?

We can be confident that the Gospel writers accurately depict the events of Yeshua's life, since it is recorded that even they were baffled by His suffering and death. They had different ideas of what the Messiah would do when He came, and so they could not understand much of what occurred as the *fulfillment* of Old Covenant prophecy. It was only *after* Yeshua's resurrection that these men were able to see how all the events of His life *and* death were spoken of by the prophets of old.

Now, the point of all this is simple: If the disciples were going to *rewrite* Yeshua's life story as a witness to their own people, why didn't they make it line up with some of the more "orthodox" Jewish expectations? Why did they make it run contrary to much of the popular feeling of the day? And why did they write a story that would surely go against the grain? Simple! It was just as Peter told the Jewish authorities who challenged him: "For we cannot help speaking about what we have seen and heard" (Acts 4:20). They were true eye-witnesses; they saw it all. They could only give it to us the way it happened to them.

As to the statement that, according to the New Covenant account of the life of Yeshua, He did not really fulfill any truly Messianic prophecies, one might well ask, "Messianic prophecies according to whom?" According to one statement in the Talmud (Sanhedrin 99a), *all* the prophets prophesied of the days of the Messiah, a statement echoed by Peter in Acts 3:22–24. Who says that Isaiah 2:1–4, speaking of the days of universal peace, *is* Messianic, while Isaiah 53, speaking of one man dying for the sins of the nation, is *not* Messianic? Who says that Numbers 24:17, speaking of the destruction of Israel's enemies, *is* Messianic, while Daniel 9:24–27, speaking of the death of the Anointed One (Hebrew *mashiach*), is *not* Messianic?

The only reason why certain prophecies of a suffering Savior have been considered non-Messianic by certain strands of Judaism is due to the fact that, if they were acknowledged as being

Messianic, then Yeshua would have to be the Messiah! Since He was, in fact, rejected by many rabbis, the next step was to reject as Messianic the prophecies that foretold His suffering and death.

■ *If the death of Yeshua really inaugurated the New Covenant spoken of by Jeremiah the prophet, then why hasn't it been fulfilled?*

Any covenant God makes with man has *conditions* and *goals*. First, there must be people who are willing to accept the stipulations of the covenant. Exodus 24:3 records that "when Moses went and told the people all the LORD's words and laws, they responded with one voice, 'Everything the LORD has said we will do.'" If some Israelites refused to accept God's covenant, then they would be cut off, but the covenant would still be binding and valid for those who did hear and obey.

For those people who did have a heart to follow God, the goals of the covenant would then be set forth. Exodus 19:5–6 records the *ideal goals* of the Mosaic Covenant: "Now if you obey me fully and keep my covenant, then out of all nations you will be my treasured possession. Although the whole earth is mine, you will be for me a kingdom of priests and a holy nation." Yet, even though this promise has never been fulfilled in the history of our nation, no one would dare question the validity and the authority of the Torah; it is *we* who have failed to keep our part of the bargain.

Those who have accepted the New Covenant's stipulations, ratified with Yeshua's own blood (Matt. 26:28), can bear witness that the promises and goals of the New Covenant are being fulfilled in them. God's law is now written in their minds and in their hearts, and the LORD has forgiven their iniquity, and remembers their sins no more (see Jeremiah 31:33–34, verses 32–33 in some versions). One day, when all Israel turns to Messiah Yeshua, the New Covenant will reach its fulfillment in the people as a whole. Until then, the *goals* of the New Covenant are being fulfilled in those who willingly accept its *conditions*.

THE MESSIAH

■ *Judaism doesn't believe in a divine Messiah.*

Judaism does believe in an *exalted* Messiah, higher than Abraham, higher than Moses, and higher than David (see, for example, the Midrash to Is. 53:12). And, according to Psalm 110:1, the LORD would say to Messiah (David's LORD), "Sit at my right hand until I make your enemies a footstool for your feet." Also, based on Jeremiah 23:6, some early rabbis offered the opinion that one of Messiah's names would be Yahweh. And Judaism does teach the *preexistence* of the Messiah, as one created before the worlds began.

More importantly, the Hebrew Scriptures clearly teach the divine nature of the Messiah. According to Isaiah 9:6 (9:5 in some versions), the King whose government and rule would have no end would be called "Wonderful Counselor, Mighty God, Everlasting Father, Prince of Peace." Although some Jewish interpreters tried to refer this passage to Hezekiah, king of Judah from about 715–687 B.C.E., he clearly was *not* the one described by Isaiah. His kingdom most definitely did come to an end, and, as a mere man, he could hardly be called *'el gibbor*, "Mighty God." In fact, "Mighty God" is used as a title of the LORD Himself in Isaiah 10:21! Modern Jewish translations of Isaiah 9:6 (9:5) that seek to soften the clear statement of Messiah's deity must ignore the most obvious meaning of the original Hebrew text.

■ *Judaism doesn't believe in a suffering Messiah.*

Although this statement is commonly made, there is almost no truth to it. The Talmud records the teaching of more than one rabbi to the effect that Messiah son of Joseph (Hebrew—*mashiach ben Yoseph*) would suffer and die in the great war that would precede the reign of Messiah son of David (Hebrew—*mashiach ben David*). In fact, Zechariah 12:10, which says, "They will look on me, the one they have pierced," quoted with reference to the death of Yeshua in the New Covenant, is applied to Messiah ben Joseph in the Rabbinic writings! It is also noteworthy that Isaiah 52:13–53:12, the clearest prophecy of a suffering Savior found in the Old Covenant Scriptures, is applied by the Targum to the Messiah, and Jewish exegesis up until approximately 550 C.E. interpreted this section almost exclusively with reference to the Messiah. Since then, the idea of a suffering Messiah has been present in many forms of Judaism, and descriptions of the Messiah's sufferings are especially rich in medieval mystical Jewish literature.

■ *Judaism doesn't believe that the Messiah will come twice.*

As noted above, the Talmud mentions *two* Messiahs, one who will suffer and die, and one who will rule and reign. Yet the Hebrew Scriptures know only *one* Messiah, descended from David. Therefore, rather than creating a *second* Messiah descended from a *different* tribe, the New Covenant writers correctly saw that there would be only *one* Messiah who would come *twice*. His first coming would be to fulfill the prophecies of a righteous sufferer who would pay for the sins of the world. His second coming would be to establish His reign of peace on the earth.

Also, statements such as "*Judaism doesn't believe...*" are often totally misleading, seeing that from one Jewish group to another there may be totally different beliefs on such important subjects as the Messiah, life after death, oral law, and even God Himself! Thus, one can find within Judaism the opinion that Messiah was created before the world began, and He has been waiting in every generation to be revealed; or, Messiah has *already been on earth* in every generation, waiting to be revealed; or, Messiah will come when the world is totally righteous; or, Messiah will come when the world is totally wicked; or, Messiah is more than a mere man; or, Messiah is only a mere man; or, Messiah is a concept; or, Messiah is a myth. Therefore, to say that "Judaism doesn't believe in a suffering Messiah, or in a Messiah who comes twice," is to give the false impression that Judaism has one set of beliefs regarding the person and work of the Messiah, and that these beliefs absolutely exclude the notion of a suffering Messiah or of a Messiah who would come twice.

■ *The Messiah is David's son. If Yeshua were really born of a virgin, then Joseph was not His father and He is really not a descendant of David. Therefore, Yeshua cannot be the Messiah.*

According to Yeshua's own words, the Messiah was at one and the same time David's *son* and David's Lord (see Matt. 22:41–46), and the New Covenant is careful to show how the natural son of David could also be the spiritual Son of God. Thus, Matthew's genealogy provides the *royal* and *legal* descent of Yeshua carried through His adoptive father Joseph, while Luke's genealogy provides His *natural* and *physical* descent through Miriam His mother. In this way, the virgin-born Son of God, greater than David, has become the royal Messiah, descended from David. Therefore, rather than the virgin birth presenting a problem for the Messiahship of Yeshua, it actually provides a proof.

■ *Yeshua cannot be the Messiah, because He is a descendant of King Jehoiachin. God cursed both this king and his offspring, saying that none of his descendants would ever sit on the throne of David.*

This argument can be answered in two very simple ways. First, it must be noted that Yeshua is *not* a natural, physical descendant of Jehoiachin (also called Jeconiah or Coniah), but only a legal descendant. Thus, only Matthew traces Yeshua's lineage through this king, while Luke's genealogy follows a different line. (Note carefully: the Shealtiel and Zerubbabel of Matthew 1:12 are probably *not* the same as the Shealtiel and Zerubbabel of Luke 3:27. This can be seen by noting that the name of Shealtiel's father in Matthew 1:12 is none other than Jeconiah, while in Luke 3:27,

Shealtiel's father is Neri. Thus, Luke's genealogy of Yeshua does *not* include Jeconiah.) Therefore, even if all of Jehoiachin's physical descendants *were* cursed, Yeshua would not have actually been under that curse.

More important, however, is that the Hebrew Scriptures plainly show that God did *not* curse all of Jehoiachin's descendants, but only his immediate offspring. In other words, God was not declaring that, for all time, none of Jehoiachin's descendants would ever sit on David's throne, but rather that his sons *who were then alive* would not rule. According to Jeremiah 22:24, God said: "Even if you, Jehoiachin...were a signet ring on my right hand, I would pull you off." And then in verse 30 He commanded: "Record this man as if childless, a man who will not prosper in his lifetime, for none of his offspring will prosper, none will sit on the throne of David or rule anymore in Judah."

Apparently, there were Jews living in Babylonian exile who hoped that their people would soon break the yoke of the Babylonians, allowing either Coniah (i.e., Jehoiachin) or one of his sons to reassume the rule in Jerusalem. Jeremiah categorically stated that this could not be, for seventy years of captivity were determined for the Jewish nation, and neither Jehoiachin nor his sons would rule again. But, two generations later, Zerubbabel, *Jehoiachin's grandson*, became governor of Judah, *and the Messianic promises were renewed through him.* Thus, the prophecy that God would shake heaven and earth and overthrow the Gentile kingdoms was spoken to Zerubbabel (Hag. 2:21–22), and in the very next verse the LORD declared: "'I will take you, my servant Zerubbabel...and I will make you like my signet ring [that's right, a signet ring! Coniah, even if he were a signet ring on God's hand, was rejected. Zerubbabel would actually *be* a signet ring to the LORD], for I have chosen you,' declares the LORD Almighty." In addition to all this, Zerubbabel became so famous in later Jewish literature that he is even mentioned in a Hanukkah prayer ("Well nigh had I perished, when Babylon's end drew near; through Zerubbabel I was saved after seventy years")!

It is impossible that Zerubbabel, Coniah's grandson, was under the curse, since he did in fact prosper (the curse said, "*none* of his [i.e., Coniah's] offspring will prosper"); and, as a son of David, he did govern the Jewish people. It is altogether fitting, then, that Matthew traces the royal line of Yeshua through Jeconiah (i.e., Jehoiachin), since the promises to David were renewed and confirmed in Zerubbabel, his grandson.

The Atonement

■ *The notion that we Jews need a blood atonement is completely wrong. First, even the book of Leviticus indicates that at certain times flour was accepted for an atonement, while Exodus 30 refers to "atonement money" and Numbers 31 mentions jewelry being offered for atonement. The prophets indicated clearly that God did not want blood sacrifices, and the rabbis have taught that God is satisfied today with prayer, repentance, and good deeds.*

Until the Temple was destroyed in 70 C.E., Jewish teaching emphasized the necessity of blood atonement. According to the Talmud, "There is not atonement (*kapparah*) without the blood" (Yoma 5a; Zebahim 6a; Menahot 93b). It is recognized by Jewish and Christian scholars alike that the New Covenant emphasis on blood atonement is based on *Jewish* beliefs of the day. And, although many Jews today think that it is the New Covenant writers who cited Leviticus 17:11 to prove that God required blood atonement, it is actually the *rabbis* of the Talmud who quoted this verse in this way! They recognized that, because "the life of a creature is in the blood," God gave it upon the altar to make atonement for His people. "It is the blood that makes atonement for one's life" (Lev. 17:11).

Blood sacrifices formed the main part of the ancient Israelite

Temple service, and according to Leviticus 16, on the Day of Atonement (Yom Kippur) *the Holy Place itself*, as well as the High Priest and all the people of Israel, were to be cleansed by the *blood* of a sacrificial goat. On the eve of Israel's exodus from Egypt, it was the *blood* of the Passover (*pesach*) lamb, put upon the two doorposts and lintel of the house, that would be a sign to the destroying angel, and the LORD said, "And when I see the *blood*, I will pass over you" (Ex. 12:13). Even the giving of the Torah at Mount Sinai was ratified with the shedding of *blood* ("This is *the blood of the covenant* that the LORD has made with you in accordance with all these words"—Ex. 24:8, and the Aramaic Targum to this verse reads: "And Moses took the blood and poured it on the altar *as atonement for the people...*").

It is with good reason that the Letter to the Hebrews says that "the law requires that nearly everything be cleansed with blood, *and without the shedding of blood there is no forgiveness*" (Heb. 9:22), since the central importance of the blood, and, in particular, the blood of atonement, is clearly seen in the Tanakh. Any other system of atonement that does not include the blood is not biblical, and any other system of atonement that fails to offer *substitutionary* atonement, i.e., an innocent sacrificial victim dying on behalf of a guilty sinner, is not able to provide real forgiveness of sins.

How then do we account for references to flour offerings and "atonement money" in the Torah? The answers again are simple. According to Leviticus 5:11–13, a poor Israelite who was unable to bring the required trespass offering of a lamb, goat, turtledoves or pigeons could bring instead an offering of fine flour. According to verse 12, the priest will "take a handful of it [i.e., the flour] as a memorial portion, *and burn it on the altar on top of the offerings made to the LORD by fire.*" Then (verse 13) "the priest will make atonement for him." In other words, the priest, in his capacity as mediator for the people, *and having mingled the flour with the blood that was already upon the altar*, would make atonement for his fellow Israelite. Nowhere is it written that "the flour will make atonement," or that "the life of a creature is in the flour." Rather, the whole basis for atonement remained in the sacrificial blood that was upon the altar.

The references to "atonement money" actually have nothing to do with atonement for sins. One example is found in Exodus 30:11–16, where every male Israelite who was to be counted in the census was to pay a *kopher* ("a ransom"; see Ex. 21:30—the owner of a goring ox that killed a man would have to pay a *kopher*, i.e., a fixed amount of ransom money). Since the taking of a census was considered to be a dangerous enterprise (according to 2 Sam. 24, when David numbered Israel, a plague broke out among the people), God told the Israelites to contribute an offering to the Tabernacle, *so that no plague would break out among them.*

Thus, the *kopher* here had to do with *protection from a plague*, and not forgiveness of sins or personal atonement. In fact, the expression in verse 15, "to atone for your lives," should really be translated as "to pay a *kopher* (ransom) for your souls." This is also the best way to translate Numbers 31:50, since the reference to the children of Israel offering gold jewelry to the LORD again has nothing to do with atonement. Having just counted the soldiers who had gone into battle with Midian (again, they had taken a *census*!), the officers decided to offer some of the spoil to God and thus, to pay a *kopher* for their souls. What connection is there between any of these narratives and the concept of personal atonement or forgiveness of sins?

As to the belief that "the prophets indicate clearly that God doesn't want blood sacrifices," it is clear from reading the prophets' own words that what they really opposed were *empty* sacrifices and *vain* offerings. If one wishes to say that the prophets wanted to *abolish* the sacrificial system, then one would also have to say that the prophets wanted to abolish the Sabbath! (See Is. 1:13: "Stop bringing *meaningless offerings*!. . .New Moons,

Sabbaths, and convocations—I cannot bear your evil assemblies.")

The prophets taught that sacrifices without mercy and justice were vain, and that bringing an offering without a repentant and contrite heart was unacceptable. Both of these themes are constantly reiterated in the New Covenant, and one of Yeshua's favorite texts was Hosea 6:6: "For I desire mercy, not sacrifice, and acknowledgement of God rather than burnt offerings" (see, e.g., Matt. 12:7). In fact, when Yeshua gave the Great Commission, He said that "*repentance and forgiveness of sins* will be preached in his name to all nations..." (Luke 24:47). Without repentance, the sacrifice of Yeshua will do the sinner no good.

When the Temple was destroyed in 70 C.E., the rabbis instituted what they thought were other forms of atonement, such as prayer, good deeds and charity. They found support for this in verses such as Hosea 14:2 (verse 3 in some versions) which states poetically, "That we may offer the fruit of our lips." Yet, while the Bible sometimes describes prayer, repentance and worship with "sacrifice imagery," it never implies that these things were to take the place of the sacrifices themselves.

Thus, in Psalm 51, after stating that "the sacrifices of God are a broken spirit" (v. 17), David says: "Then there will be righteous sacrifices, whole burnt offerings to delight you; then bulls will be offered on your altar" (v. 19). Another good example is Psalm 141 where David asks that his *prayer* be set before God as *incense*, and that the *lifting up of his hands* be as the *evening sacrifice*. Yet no one would suggest that King David, who brought the ark of God to Jerusalem, and who desired to build a permanent "house" for the LORD, wanted to abolish incense or the evening sacrifice!

The rabbis have taught us much that is beautiful regarding prayer, repentance and good deeds. Yet, as beautiful as this teaching is, it provides us with no suitable replacement for the blood of atonement. To this very day, there are still orthodox Jews who, recognizing their need for an atonement sacrifice, kill a chicken on Yom Kippur, wave it around their heads and say: "This is my substitute! This is my atonement!" What a sad testimony to our people's lack of true forgiveness outside of God's way through Messiah! And what clear evidence of the fact that, with the Temple destroyed, traditional Judaism offers no *new* covenant, *ratified with blood*, and acceptable in the sight of God.

■ *What did the Jews living in Babylonian exile, before Yeshua died and with no sacrifices to offer, do for atonement?*

It is significant that the Jews who were in exile in Babylon longed for the days when the Temple would be rebuilt, and they fully recognized that it was *because of their sin* that the Temple had been destroyed (see Dan. 9:1–19). Interestingly enough, scholars believe that it was during this very time of exile that the teaching of Isaiah's *Suffering Servant* came to prominence. The hope of the Messiah was coming alive, and the Jewish people were being directed to the One who would bring to fulfillment the system of Old Covenant blood sacrifices by offering up Himself. By the time the Second Temple was destroyed in 70 C.E., He had already come and done His work.

The Jews in Babylonian captivity could look forward to the coming of the Deliverer who would be cut "off, but not for himself" (Dan. 9:26, text note). Today, our Jewish people can look back to the One who paid the ransom for our souls.

■ *Even if we admit that we need the blood, we still can't believe in Yeshua. God wanted the blood of a goat or a lamb, not a person.*

The writer to the Hebrews stated that "it is impossible for the blood of bulls and goats to take away sins" (Heb. 10:4). Obviously a just God could not accept the death of an innocent and ignorant animal for the payment of human sins. Rather, as Rashi stated in his commentary on Leviticus 17:11, there was a principle involved: "Because the life of the flesh of every creature is dependent on the blood, I have therefore given it [upon the altar] to make atonement for the life of man. Let life come and atone for life!"

God was teaching His people that sin deserved death (see Deut. 24:16, 30:15, and Ezek. 18:4). Yet, because He was merciful and compassionate, He provided a way of escape—the life of an innocent victim would take the place of the sinner. Passages such as Isaiah 53 make it clear, however, that these sacrifices were only a great object lesson pointing forward to the coming of the One who would "do away with sin by the sacrifice of himself" (Heb. 9:26). His blood alone would provide an acceptable sacrifice for the sins of the world.

On the holiest day of the year, Yom Kippur, the High Priest would perform a very significant ritual. He would take two goats and present them before the LORD (Lev. 16:7). One goat was to be killed, and its blood offered to "make atonement for the Most Holy Place because of the uncleanness and rebellion of the Israelites, whatever their sins have been" (verse 16). Then he would take the second goat, which was still alive, and, laying both his hands on its head, he would "confess over it all the wickedness and rebellion of the Israelites—all their sins—and put them on the goat's head" (verse 21). He would then send it away into the wilderness, where the goat would "carry on itself all their sins to a solitary place" (verse 22).

God had devised a plan whereby sin would not only be *atoned for*, but it would actually be *removed.* Justice would then be satisfied, for sin would be punished. And yet mercy would be fulfilled, for the sinner would be forgiven. Thus, in physically graphic and literal terms, the LORD was pointing forward to the death of Messiah, who, in one act, would provide the blood of atonement and remove our sins far from us.

And it is this very concept, viz., *that the suffering of the righteous could provide atonement for the sins of the world*, which is so well known in Judaism. Thus, the Zohar states so clearly that, because

> *the children of the world are members of one another, when the Holy One desires to give healing to the world, He smites one just man amongst them, and for his sake heals all the rest. Whence do we learn this? From the saying, "He was wounded for our transgressions, bruised for our iniquities," i.e., by the letting of His blood—as when a man bleeds his arm—there was healing for us—for all the members of the body. In general a just person is only smitten in order to procure healing and atonement for a whole generation.*

Could one ask for a clearer statement of the substitutionary death of Yeshua, by whose wounds we are healed?

The Law (Torah)

■ *The Torah is forever, every jot and tittle, and only traditional Jews keep it. In fact, even the so-called New Covenant of Jeremiah 31 says that God will put the Torah in our hearts. Therefore, since Yeshua abolished the Torah, He cannot be the Messiah.*

Yeshua came to *fulfill* the Torah, not to abolish it, and in Him alone can it truly be said that "the Torah is forever." The clearest example of this truth is found with regard to the rituals of the Tabernacle and the Levitical priesthood, which formed such a large part of the Mosaic legislation. Over and over it was stated that these institutions and their governing laws were "eternal" (see, e.g., Ex. 27:21, 28:43, 29:9, 29:28, 40:15). But with the Temple destroyed, how could the Jewish people observe these commandments? Without a sanctuary, how could there be legitimate sacrifices, acceptable to God?

The New Covenant provides the answer, for not only did Yeshua foretell the destruction of the Temple forty years in advance (see, e.g., Luke 19:42–44), but, by His substitutionary death on the cross, He fulfilled the demands of the Law's sacrificial system. When the Temple did in fact fall, the followers of Yeshua had no problem, *since they did not have to invent alternative means of atonement.* Their sacrifice for sins had already been made.

As far as traditional Judaism is concerned, it has had no sacrifices since 70 C.E.; but those who recognize Yeshua as Messiah have enjoyed His once-for-all sacrifice for every generation. Thus, rather than Yeshua *abolishing* the sacrificial system, He has brought it to fulfillment. In the same way, His identification as the Lamb of God has effectively deepened and underscored the Passover message of liberation from bondage, and Messianic Jews can celebrate this holiday with greater fervor and conviction than ever before. Through Moses they have been delivered from the hand of Pharaoh, and through Yeshua they have been redeemed from the power of sin!

Another example is seen in the fact that the *priesthood of all Israel* was established as a goal of the Torah (Ex. 19:6). The Pharisees sought to realize this goal by developing a system that required every Jew to live with the same ritual cleanliness as a consecrated priest. Unfortunately, this only resulted in new regulations and laws, without bringing the people into a truly priestly ministry. Yet now, through Yeshua the Messiah, all New Covenant believers are "being built into a spiritual house to be *a holy priesthood, offering spiritual sacrifices acceptable to God...*" (1 Pet. 2:5). The New Covenant community has become the very Temple of God (see Eph. 2:19–22), and *every believing member* has direct access into the holy presence of the King!

As far as the *ethical* commandments of the Law are concerned, Yeshua always brought out the *deepest* meanings of God's righteous requirements, and He refused to allow following the LORD to degenerate into a mere outward formality. One key feature of the New Covenant as prophesied by Jeremiah was that the Torah would be written in our *hearts*. Thus, rather than destroying and nullifying the Law, Yeshua planted it in our hearts and gave us the ability through the Spirit not only to hear, but also to obey.

As for the argument that while Yeshua did not actually abolish the Law, He did *change* it, the question may be asked, "Doesn't Jewish tradition teach that when Messiah comes, He will give new commandments or a new Torah?" In other words, while the righteous principles of the Law will never change, won't some of the earthbound regulations be affected? And if this is possible, could not Yeshua *as Messiah* institute certain "New Commandments," since He had brought about the fulfillment of Torah's demands in His perfect life and sacrificial death? This being the case, is it even accurate to speak of Yeshua's *changing* the Law?

Paul, James and the other early followers of Yeshua were known as observant Jews who were zealous for the Law (Acts 21:20–25). What better proof could there be that Yeshua *in no way* sought to contradict, nullify, or abrogate the commandments of God? It is ironic that today, when Messianic Jews want to worship on Saturday, celebrate the feasts and circumcise their sons as children of Abraham, they are called deceptive and hypocritical!

While there are some who argue that in order for Jeremiah's New Covenant prophecy to be truly fulfilled, God would have to place the *whole Torah* in our hearts, this argument is based on a misconception of the biblical meaning of Torah. Actually, although the Hebrew word *torah* is generally taken as referring to the first Five Books of the Bible (the Pentateuch), and while many Jews understand every reference to *torah* in the Scriptures as meaning *God's entire revelation to His Jewish people*, the fact is that *torah* has a variety of meanings in the Tanakh.

In the sense of "*the* Torah," it can be a synonym for the first Five Books. Yet, more often than not, it simply means "teaching," "instruction," "law," or "regulation." Therefore, when Jeremiah prophesied that under the New Covenant, God would put the *To-*

rah in the hearts of Israel and Judah, he was saying that God's teaching would be planted within the believer, and that the revelation of the LORD would, by the Spirit (see Ezek. 36:25–27), be internalized. He was not saying that *the traditional Jewish Torah*, consisting of Mishnah and Talmud, would automatically be placed in the hearts of the partakers of this covenant!

Such a concept would not only have been strange to Jeremiah's ears, it would have been totally alien, since the concept of "traditional interpretation of the Law" had not even come into existence! And, although traditional Jews claim that the "oral law" was revealed to Moses, almost all modern Jewish scholars will admit that the vast part of the oral law did not even exist before the days of Yeshua. It is therefore with every right that Messianic Jews claim to be the true heirs of Moses and the Prophets, children of the New Covenant. We do not lean on later Jewish tradition. We place our feet firmly on the written revelation of God.

■ *According to the Law, Yeshua was a false prophet, and those who follow Him are guilty of the worst kind of idolatry: making God into a man!*

Deuteronomy 13:1–3 says:

> *If a prophet, or one who foretells by dreams appears among you and announces to you a miraculous sign or wonder, and if the sign or wonder of which he has spoken takes place, and he says, "Let us follow other gods" (gods you have not known) "and let us worship them," you must not listen to the words of that prophet or dreamer. The LORD your God is testing you to find out whether you love him with all your heart and with all your soul.*

According to these criteria, Yeshua can only be classified as a true and faithful prophet, since the entire object of His earthly ministry was to bring glory and honor to His Father, the God of Israel. When asked which was the first and greatest commandment, Jesus answered: "The most important one...is this: 'Hear O Israel, the Lord our God, the Lord is one. Love the Lord your God with all your heart and with all your soul and with all your mind and with all your strength' " (Mark 12:29–30). Matthew records that when the crowds saw the great miracles that He did, "they praised the God of Israel" (Matt. 15:31). Over and again, Yeshua pointed the people to God.

How then could it be said that Yeshua Himself was God? And doesn't this in fact make God into man?

First, it should be emphasized that both traditional Jews as well as Messianic Jews would agree that "God is not a man" (Num. 23:19), and that for God in His totality to become man would mean that God would cease to be God. And yet Judaism has often asked the question of how God, who is an infinite spiritual Being, can come into fellowship with man, who is a finite physical (and spiritual) being. In answer to this question, various streams of Jewish teaching have offered some different solutions, and yet all of them have this one thought in common—one way or another, God condescended to the level of man.

Some rabbis taught that God, the perfect Spirit, reached down to man, the imperfect earthling, by means of successive emanations (Hebrew, *sephirot*) of His being. In other words, He revealed Himself in successive stages or spheres, until, at the lowest sphere, He was able to be perceived by man. Others believed that He revealed Himself to man through His Divine Word (Aramaic, *memra'*).

Each of these concepts gives us insights into the New Covenant portrayal of Yeshua as Son of Man and Son of God. First, the idea that there are different spheres or emanations in God is *similar* to the idea of the Trinity: God, who is One, exists in the Persons of the Father, Son, and Holy Spirit. It is in this way alone that He reveals Himself to man. Thus, Yeshua (the Son) came down to earth to reveal the Father to the world. This is what He meant when He said, "I came from the Father and entered the world: now I am leaving the world and going back to the Father" (John 16:28); and, "No one knows the Father except the Son and those to whom the Son chooses to reveal him" (Matt. 11:27).

There is also much Jewish teaching that speaks of the Shekinah, *the Divine Presence itself*, going into exile with the Jewish people. According to this concept, God cannot be "whole" again until His people return from their physical and spiritual exile, since the rabbis saw in the Shekinah the "motherly" aspect of God, suffering with her children in foreign lands. Similarly, the New Covenant teaches us that God, in the Person of the Son, has joined Himself with man—Yeshua is thus wholly God and wholly man. As the Son, the One who proceeded forth from the Father, He was the "image of the invisible God" to us. As Man, He lived a perfectly righteous life and died for our sins, thereby becoming the "new" or "second" Adam.

As for the revelation of God by means of His *memra'* (Word), Jewish teaching understands that, because God is infinite and totally above man, He can only interact with us by His Word. Thus, rather than God Himself "touching" this earth, He does it by means of His *memra'*. Of course, readers of the New Covenant will immediately think of John's description of Yeshua as "the Word" (Greek, *logos*) Who was *with* God in the beginning, and yet at the same time *was* God. And, although "no one has ever seen God,...God the One and Only, who is at the Father's side," has declared God to us (John 1:18). We learn about the Father by means of His Word! And, just as the Hebrew Scriptures declare that God created all things *by His Word* (see Gen. 1 and Ps. 33:6–9), so also the New Covenant teaches us that it is through Yeshua that all things were created, and it is by Him that all things consist (Col. 1:16, 17).

From all this we can learn two important facts. First, while Judaism has consistently taught that God alone is the Savior, it has also taught that, in a sense, "man must save himself." Both of these concepts, rooted as they are in the Scriptures, are fulfilled in Yeshua: as man, He broke the power of sin over man and paid the penalty for our disobedience; as God, He alone is the means by which we can be saved, since man without God will always turn away.

Second, although the New Covenant concept of the Trinity does *not* allow for different *levels* of deity (although the Jewish mystical concept of the *sephirot* seems to view the divine "emanations" in this way), the consistent emphasis in the Scriptures is that the *Father* is God and *Yeshua* is the Messiah. Thus, Paul could write that when all things are made subject to Yeshua the Son, "then the Son himself will be made subject to him who put everything under him, so that God may be all in all" (1 Cor. 15:28).

It is clear, then, that, rather than having a coarse and idolatrous view of God, the New Covenant has explained to us the real way by which God could remain the high and lofty Holy One, sitting on His heavenly throne, while at the same time, as the Savior of the world, He was reaching down to the lowliest sinner. And it is through the earthly ministry of Yeshua that countless millions of people around the world have "turned to God from idols to serve the living and true God" (1 Thess. 1:9). He alone is the Savior, and He alone will bring the nations to God.

KEYS TO UNDERSTANDING MESSIANIC PROPHECY BY DR. MICHAEL BROWN

"You don't know what you're talking about!"

"You're completely misinterpreting Isaiah!"

"This verse has absolutely *nothing* to do with your Jesus! The fact is, it's not even a Messianic prophecy!"

"As for the *real* Messianic prophecies, Jesus fulfilled none of them."

These are some common arguments used by those who do not believe in Yeshua as their Messiah. Listed below are important keys and principles that will help you to see that, in fact, Yeshua fulfilled the prophecies of the Hebrew Scriptures.

1) MESSIANIC PROPHECIES ARE NOT CLEARLY IDENTIFIED AS SUCH.

There is not a single verse in the entire Hebrew Bible that is specifically identified as a Messianic prophecy. Nowhere do the Scriptures say, "The next paragraph contains a prediction of the Messiah!" Thus, whether or not one accepts a certain passage as Messianic depends largely on how one understands the person and work of the Messiah.

For example, if someone believes that the Messiah will be a king who will bring peace to the earth, he will probably interpret

Isaiah 11 as a Messianic prophecy. But he will not interpret Isaiah 53 in a Messianic way *because it does not fit his preconceived notion of what the Messiah will do.* And so, when I point to Isaiah 53, he will confidently say to me, "But that is not a Messianic prophecy!"

How can I answer this argument? Just by asking two simple questions: "Who says Isaiah 53 is *not* Messianic while Isaiah 11 *is* Messianic? Who says your interpretation is right?" In other words, I want to help him see that his understanding of Messianic prophecy is based on *traditional bias* as opposed to *objective scriptural truth.* Maybe it is *he* who has brought preconceived notions to the text. If he is open to dialogue, I can take things a step further and ask, "Are you sure your picture of the Messiah is correct? Maybe you are missing some of the pieces to the puzzle! How do you know that Messiah hasn't already come?" And from there I can show him the way!

2) The Messianic hope in Israel developed gradually.

Messianic prophecies were not clearly identified as such because they were not initially understood as referring to *the Messiah.* Also, the Hebrew word *mashiach* (Messiah), which literally means "anointed one," almost never refers to *the Messiah* in the Hebrew Bible. Instead, it refers to the anointed king (like Saul or David), the anointed high priest (like Aaron), or even an "anointed" (chosen) foreign ruler (like Cyrus).

Let's apply this to the Messianic hope in Israel. David was a great king, a *mashiach* of the Lord; so was his son Solomon, who had a wonderful reign of peace. Many of the Psalms were written for them or about them: Psalm 72, which is a prayer for Solomon; Psalm 2, which celebrates the coronation of the king; or Psalm 45, which commemorates the royal wedding ceremony. And when all was well, God's people recognized no need for *the Messiah.*

But when Israel's kings began to fail, when there were no more Davids or Solomons, and when the Jewish people were exiled from their Land, they began to realize their need for a special *mashiach*, supernaturally anointed by God. And what do you think happened when they went back and reread the Psalms? They began to see the Messianic significance of the verses! They recognized, for example, that Psalm 2, which prophesied *the worldwide dominion* of the LORD's anointed, was *not* fulfilled by David, Solomon, or any other king. It could only be fulfilled by *the Messiah*. And so, little by little, they began to understand the Messianic hope.

3) MANY BIBLICAL PROPHECIES ARE FULFILLED GRADUALLY.

This key principle applies to *all types* of prophecy, whether Messianic or not. This is also implied by the word "fulfill": the prophet's words had to be "filled up to the full" to be "fulfilled."

Ezekiel, *living in the Babylonian exile*, prophesied that his people should return from their captivity. The fulfillment *began* in 538 B.C.E., when the first group of exiles returned to Judah; it has *continued* in this century with the return of the Jewish people to the Land; and it *will reach fulfillment* when Jesus comes back and gathers His scattered people from every corner of the globe. Over 2500 years and still being fulfilled!

Now let's look at a Messianic prophecy. Zechariah prophesies that when Israel's King comes, He will be "righteous and having salvation, gentle and riding on a donkey.... His rule will extend from sea to sea, and from the River to the ends of the earth" (9:9–10). If you show this to a rabbi, he will probably say, "It's clear that Jesus hasn't fulfilled it!"

How would I respond? Simply by explaining to him that the prophecy *is presently being fulfilled* (i.e., it is in the ongoing process of fully coming to pass): Jesus *came* as the prophet foretold, "righteous and having salvation, gentle and riding on a donkey"; *every day* the number of individuals over whom He reigns as King continues to increase (countless millions from every country!) and *in the future*, when He returns, He will completely establish His rule.

4) THE PROPHETS SAW THE MESSIAH COMING ON THE IMMEDIATE HORIZON OF HISTORY.

Have you ever stood on top of a mountain and looked across to another mountain peak? The mountains appear to be next to each other, even though there is a huge valley in between. It is the same with biblical prophecy. *The prophets saw the future through a telescope.* Things far away in time appeared close. They did not realize that centuries would come and go between their initial prediction and its actual fulfillment. In fact, to the prophets, the expression "at the end of days" could have meant "right around the corner"!

Why is this principle important to understand with regard to Messianic prophecy? Because believers in Yeshua are often accused of taking a verse "out of context." We are told, "That prophecy applied to Isaiah's day 2700 years ago. It certainly does not refer to Jesus!" But did it *really* apply to Isaiah's day, or was it an example of prophecy being telescopic? Did Isaiah see the coming of the Messiah (i.e., a great deliverer) *in the context of his very own day*?

Let's look at Isaiah 9:1–7 (8:23–9:6 in some Bibles) where it is predicted that the yoke of the enemy (i.e., Assyria) would be broken by the son of David *who was already born.* And this son of David would have an everlasting kingdom of peace. When was Assyria crushed? 2600 years ago. Who was born shortly before that time? Hezekiah. Did *he* fulfill the prophecy? Obviously not! But the prophet saw the coming of the future Davidic ruler as if it were about to happen in his very own day.

Watch carefully for prophecies like this, since they are extremely common. In fact, this key to prophetic interpretation is really a summary of the first three principles just given. If you go back and read them again, things will begin to fall into place for you.

5) It is important to read every prophecy in its overall context in Scripture.

Do the New Covenant writers take Old Covenant verses out of context, or are they faithful to the meaning of the text? In Matthew 1:23, Isaiah 7:14 is applied to the birth of Jesus (the virgin [or, maiden] will bear a son and call his name Immanuel). But is this quotation faithful to Isaiah? How can Matthew apply *a sign given to King Ahaz about 734 B.C.E.* to the birth of Yeshua over 700 years later? How could this be a relevant sign?

Consider the context of Isaiah chapters 7–11. Judah was being attacked by Israel and Aram. These nations wanted to replace Ahaz, who represented the house of David (see Is. 7:2, 13), with their own man named Ben Tabeel. *This would mean the end of Davidic rule in Judah.* Yet when Ahaz would not ask God for a sign, God gave him His own: a child named Immanuel (meaning "God is with us") would be born and within a few years, before the child was very old, Judah's enemies would be destroyed.

Who was this Immanuel? Obviously a child to be born to the house of David in place of faithless Ahaz, a son who would be a token of the fact that God was with His people (in other words, good news for the nation and bad news for Ahaz!). But is his birth ever mentioned in the book of Isaiah? No! In fact, the birth of Isaiah's son Maher-Shalal-Hash-Baz in Isaiah 8:1–4 *seems to take its place as a time-setter* (read Is. 7:14–16 and 8:3–4; before Maher-Shalal-Hash-Baz would be very old, Judah's enemies would be destroyed—just what was said about Immanuel!).

What happened to Immanuel? Nothing is clearly said. But what is clearly said in Isaiah 9:6–7 (9:5–6 in some Bibles) and 11:1–16 is that there will come forth a rod from Jesse (David's father) who will rule the nations in righteousness.

And this was Matthew's context! He was reading Isaiah 7–11 in full! Thus he quotes Isaiah 7:14 in Matthew 1:23; Isaiah 9:1–2 (8:23–9:1 in some Bibles) in Matthew 4:15–16; and he alludes to

Isaiah 11:1 in Matthew 2:23 (the Hebrew word for "Nazarene" resembles the Hebrew word for "branch").

Was anyone born in Isaiah's day that began to fulfill the Immanuel prophecy? We simply do not know. But of this we can be sure: Jesus, the ideal King from the house of David, and clearly the subject of the Messianic prophecies in chapters 9 and 11, is Immanuel—God with us—in the fullest sense of the word!

6) The Messiah was to be both a Priest and King.

Everyone who believes in the Messiah accepts the *royal* prophecies of the Scriptures as referring to Messiah the King. But what about the predictions of *suffering*? What do *these* verses have to do with the Messiah?

Here is an important answer! *The prophecies of suffering and death point to the priestly ministry of the Messiah, since it was the duty of the High Priest to intercede for his people and make atonement for their sins.*

Did you know that in the first century of this era there was widespread belief in the coming of a *priestly* Messianic figure as well as a *royal* Messianic figure? This belief was almost correct. There *was* to be a priest and there *was* to be a king, only these two figures were one! According to Psalm 110, the Davidic ruler was to be both priest and king. In Zechariah 6, *the crown* is placed on the head of *the High Priest* named Joshua (he is also called *Yeshua* in Ezra and Nehemiah!), who is then referred to as "the Branch," a Messianic title!

Thus, it is clear that the Messiah would have a dual role: as High Priest He would take His people's sins on Himself and intercede for them; as King He would rule and reign. Because traditional Judaism has largely forgotten the Messiah's priestly work, it has not always recognized key passages in Isaiah as referring to Him.

7) THE MESSIAH IS THE IDEAL REPRESENTATIVE OF HIS PEOPLE.

In ancient Israel, the king and his people were one. As the kings of Israel went, so went the nation. They saw themselves represented in their head.

How does this apply to the Messiah? First, the history of Israel paralleled the life of Jesus. For example, when Moses was born, Pharaoh was trying to kill Israelite baby boys, and when Jesus was born, Herod began killing Jewish baby boys. Also, both the nation of Israel as well as Jesus spent their early years in Egypt. (*That* is why Matthew quotes Hos. 11:1 in Matt. 2:15! Compare also Matt. 2:20 with Ex. 4:19.)

And because the Messiah was the ideal representative of his people, *He fulfills the words of their psalms.* Thus Psalm 22, the psalm of the righteous sufferer whom God wonderfully delivers, is not identified at all as a Messianic prophecy. Yet, to any impartial reader, it is clear that both the depth of suffering described as well as the universal effects of the deliverance can refer only to Jesus, the ideal righteous Sufferer, the representative King, the greater David. Therefore, the New Covenant writers often see the Psalms as containing Messianic prophecies, since the Messiah is seen as their ultimate, representative subject.

■

How can you put all these principles together? Every time you see a Messianic prophecy quoted in the New Covenant, look it up in the Old Covenant and read the whole section from which it is taken (this could be a paragraph, a chapter, or even more). Then, try and see which of the interpretive keys explains the quote. Remember: many times several principles are at work together!

Not only will you enrich your understanding of the Word, but you will learn to appreciate how wonderfully God has woven together the prophecies of the Messiah's coming.

ARE THE RABBIS RIGHT?
BY DR. MICHAEL BROWN

The following passages are excerpted from a special cassette entitled, "Are the Rabbis Right?" offered by the Messianic Vision.

It's often said by the rabbinic community to Christians that you cannot have a Christianity without a Christ. And it's said in somewhat of a negative way. In other words, you can have a Judaism without a Messiah, but you cannot have a Christianity without a Christ.

I don't take that as an insult. I thank God for sending us the Messiah. But I want to give you a parallel statement—you cannot have rabbinic Judaism without a rabbi. You cannot have traditional Judaism without a tradition.

According to the rabbinic teaching, quoting from an introduction to the Talmud by a famous Jewish scholar named Zevi Hirsch Chajes, "The Torah, divine instruction, is divided into two parts: the written and the unwritten law. The former, the written law, consists of the Pentateuch, which was divinely revealed to Moses at Sinai."

Everyone accepts the Pentateuch (five books of Moses) as authoritative, the written law that God gave and that formed the basis for all later Jewish thought, all later Jewish law, all later Jewish teaching. This is the foundation and I agree with this. But now Chajes goes on to say "the latter, the unwritten law, comprises expositions and interpretations which were communicated to Moses orally as a supplement to the former."

The traditional Jewish view is that God gave Moses the written law, which is often obscure and doesn't tell you everything you need to know. That was put down in writing. And then God told Moses all the other things, really hundreds and thousands of laws and interpretations and insights into the written Scriptures. He told Moses to pass them on to Joshua and then Joshua to the elders that lived in his day and then the elders to the prophets, and so on right up to Jesus' day and then after that right up to the rabbinic community to this day.

Some of those traditions got written down. That's called the Mishnah, the Talmud, and the later Jewish law codes. Other traditions were just passed on orally. But according to Chajes, "Allegiance to the authority of the said rabbinic tradition is binding upon all sons of Israel since these explanations and interpretations have come down to us by word of mouth, from generation to generation right from the time of Moses."

Those sentences that I just quoted to you are the traditional, standard view. The oral law was handed down to Moses and he handed it down, directly transmitted it, and it's been transmitted verbatim throughout all the ages.

And it says here, "They have been transmitted to us, precise, correct, unadulterated. And he who does not give his adherence to the unwritten law and the rabbinic tradition has no right to share the heritage of Israel."

Chaim Schimmel, a Jewish lawyer who wrote a book called *The Oral Law*, speaking of our Jewish people, says this, and this is very surprising: "They do not follow the literal word of the Bible, nor have they ever done so. They have been fashioned and ruled by the verbal interpretation of the written word, more particularly by the Torah, which embraces both the written and the oral law."

Now here's the problem I have with all of this. I can show you by the five books of Moses and throughout the rest of the Scripture that *there was no such thing as an authoritative oral tradition.* God made a covenant with Israel for all time based on a written word and a written word alone. Every single reference in the entire Hebrew Bible to violating the Torah of Moses is only a reference to violating the written Torah. There is never any reference to violating any oral law, oral tradition or anything. Why? Because it didn't exist. It was developed much later and then in the memory of the people was attributed to an earlier time in history.

Yet despite the lack of evidence, the rabbinic community has placed great importance on the oral law. Tractate Gittin, 60b of the Babylonian Talmud says: "The Holy One, blessed be He, did not make His covenant with Israel except by virtue of the oral law." And then in the Jerusalem Talmud, in Tractate Pe'ah, Section three, Halakhah three, a rabbi was trying to figure out which was more important, the oral law or the written law. He says: "Words were given orally and words were given in writing and I didn't know which of the two sets was the more valuable. However, from the verse, Exodus 34:27, 'According to these words have I made a covenant with you...,' we learn that those that were transmitted orally are the more valuable."

What does Exodus 34:27 have to do with the oral law? Let me read this verse to you from the New Jewish Version (all Scriptures below are from this version): "And the Lord said to Moses: Write down these commandments, for in accordance with these commandments I make a covenant with you and with Israel." Look at that. "Write down these commandments." How do they get the interpretation based on this verse that the oral law is more valuable than the written law because it explains and interprets the written law? Very simply—by a total misinterpretation of the Hebrew words translated "in accordance." The Hebrew words by themselves would mean "on the mouth." But every Hebrew scholar would agree that here the words mean "in accordance."

So God didn't say I'm making a covenant with you based on the oral law. He said I'm making a covenant with you based on what you're going to *write down.* Many times the rabbinic community accuses Messianic Jews of taking Scripture out of context and of twisting the meaning of Scripture. And I'd say with all respect to the great learning that many rabbis do have, that the foundations of rabbinic Judaism are based on misinterpretation and twisting of Scripture.

What I want to challenge you with is this: *by giving oral law a higher place than God's written Word, rabbinic tradition has usurped divine authority. Rabbinic tradition has replaced the prophetic voice. Rabbinic tradition has taken the place of a face-to-face encounter with God.*

Let me explain to you what I mean by a face-to-face encounter with God. In Deuteronomy 5:2–4, Moses is speaking to the children of Israel as they are about to enter the promised land after almost forty years of wandering in the wilderness, He says: "The LORD our God made a covenant with us at Horeb [Sinai]. It was not with our fathers that the LORD made this covenant, but with us, the living, every one of us who is here today. Face to face the Lord spoke to you on the mountain out of the fire. . . ."

You say, "Well, what does that mean?" Didn't God make a covenant with our forefathers and here Moses is saying he didn't make it with our fathers, but only with us?

Here's what it means. Moses said that God made the covenant with *us* the living. Yes, he did make a covenant with your fathers, but they're dead now. They died in the wilderness. You who heard God speak from the mountain face to face and are still alive, you are the ones He made the covenant with.

Why? Because God doesn't make covenants with dead people, but only with living people. I can't say, "Well, God made a covenant with my forefathers, therefore I am in it." No. I have to myself enter into it. I myself have to have that living experience, that living entering into the relationship of the covenant with God.

But didn't God also make a covenant with our children? Yes, but they themselves must enter into it in a living way.

When I asked an ultra-orthodox man why he lives the way he lives, the basic gist of his answer was, "Well, it's pretty good. My father did it, I learned it from him, now I'm going to teach my children and they're going to learn it from me and they're going to grow up and do the same things I do."

Have you entered into that relationship with God that Moses and the first generation of Israelites had, or have you simply mimicked what you learned and your fathers mimicked what they learned? I don't mean mimicked in a negative way, I mean following traditions that have been learned by rote. Is that what you're doing as a traditional Jew?

One of the foundations of rabbinic Judaism is that the majority rules. The only text in the Bible that is used to prove that is Exodus 23:2: "You shall neither side with the mighty to do wrong—you shall not give perverse testimony in a dispute so as to pervert it in favor of the mighty—nor shall you show deference to a poor man in his dispute." In other words, *don't follow the majority* (mighty). What the rabbis did is knock out the word "don't" and just said, "Follow the majority."

If you'll read rabbinic scholars talking about it, this verse is admittedly taken out of context and changed in meaning. Nowhere does the Bible hint at such a thing, that the majority of the leaders in the community have the right view. In fact, basically every time that you read the history of our Jewish people in the Bible, you'll see very plainly that the majority, even the majority of leaders, was almost always wrong.

"How do you know who was right or wrong?" you ask. The first thing is that we have the written word. Whoever violated or changed the meaning of the written word could not be following God. They could not be right. Not only that, God would confirm His Word with miracles, signs, and wonders. And finally, God spoke to His people through the prophets.

One of the greatest rabbis who ever lived was Moses Mamonides (1135–1204). In his introduction to his commentary on the Mishnah, he says some very startling things. He says that if someone who is a proven prophet tells you to follow the literal word of the Torah and the literal word runs contrary to the rabbinic interpretation, he's a false prophet. *That is saying that human rabbinic authority is more weighty, more powerful, more decisive than the testimony of a proven prophet following the literal word of the Scripture. If you accept this, then the plain sense of the Bible is no longer binding. You can make anything mean anything.*

The rabbi's view is that somehow or another rabbinic interpretation is the true interpretation of the written law, even when it seems to contradict what is written down. What I say is this: according to Exodus 24, verses 3–4, it says that Moses read aloud all the words that were written down in the book and that that was the covenant that the Lord made with the children of Israel. (See also Exodus 34:27.)

Joshua 1:8 says "Let not this Book of the Teaching cease from your lips, but recite it day and night, so that you may observe faithfully all that is written in it. Only then will you prosper in your undertakings and only then will you be successful." Did you get that? "Let not this *Book of the Teaching* cease from your lips. . . ." That's what God gave to the people of Israel. It's the written Torah. The oral Torah, the oral tradition was something that came in much later and violates prophetic authority.

I remember when I first believed that Jesus was the Messiah, that he had come to fulfill the promises in the Torah that God would raise up a prophet and that he was the last great prophet that God raised up to speak to Israel. I understood that he came as the fulfillment of the image of the high priest in the Torah who would stand and make sacrifice and make atonement for the sins of the people.

It says in Isaiah 53, that the righteous servant of the Lord,

> *makes the many righteous, it is their punishment that he bears; assuredly I will give him the many as his portion, he shall receive the multitude as his spoil. For he exposed himself to death and was numbered among the sinners, whereas he bore the guilt of the many and made intercession for sinners* (vs. 11b–12).

When I understood that Jesus made atonement for me, my life was radically changed. I want you to understand this great mystery, that Jesus who was exalted and recognized as the Messiah and loved and worshiped by men and women, millions and millions of them all over the world, to this day, was a Jewish carpenter who was nailed to a tree and despised by our own people. And to this day is despised by many of our own people. But He is the key. That's the mystery. He was the exalted One, He was the despised One. He is One and the same.

Are the rabbis right about Talmud? Are the rabbis right about Jesus?

BLOW THE SHOFAR FOR ALIYAH

It's time for the Jew to make Aliyah (return) to Israel. Here are ten of over 700 Scriptures where God promises the Land of Canaan to His chosen people and commands or encourages them to return to the land of Israel, which He gave to them as an everlasting inheritance.

> *Therefore this is what the Sovereign* L*ORD* *says: I will now bring Jacob back from captivity and will have compassion on all the people of Israel, and I will be zealous for my holy name. They will forget their shame and all the unfaithfulness they showed toward me when they lived in safety in their land with no one to make them afraid. When I have brought them back from the nations and have gathered them from the countries of their enemies, I will show myself holy through them in the sight of many nations. Then they will know that I am the* L*ORD* *their God, for though I sent them into exile among the nations, I will gather them to their own land, not leaving any behind. I will no longer hide my face from them, for I will pour out my Spirit on the house of Israel, declares the Sovereign* L*ORD* (Ezek. 39:25–29).

Come, O Zion! Escape, you who live in the Daughter of Babylon! (Zech. 2:7).

"I am with you and will save you," declares the L*ORD. "Though I completely destroy all the nations among which I scatter you, I will not completely destroy you. I will discipline you but only with justice; I will not let you go entirely unpunished"* (Jer. 30:11).

Come out of her, my people! Run for your lives! Run from the fierce anger of the L*ORD . . . . You who have escaped the sword, leave and do not linger! Remember the* L*ORD in a distant land and think on Jerusalem* (Jer. 51:45, 50).

Those who cling to worthless idols [comforts of Babylon] *forfeit the grace that could be theirs* (Jon. 2:8).

Shake off your dust; rise up, sit enthroned, O Jerusalem. Free yourself from the chains on your neck, O captive Daughter of Zion. For this is what the L*ORD says: "You were sold for nothing, and without money you will be redeemed"* (Is. 52:2, 3).

Set up road signs; put up guideposts. Take note of the highway, the road that you may take. Return, O Virgin Israel, return to your towns (Jer. 31:21).

"However, the days are coming," declares the L*ORD, "when men will no longer say, 'As surely as the* L*ORD lives, who brought the Israelites up out of the land of Egypt,' but they will say, 'As surely as the* L*ORD lives, who brought the Israelites up out of the land of the north and out of all the countries where he had banished them.' For I will restore them to the land I gave their forefathers. But now I will send for many*

fishermen," declares the L*ORD*, *"and they will catch them. After that I will send for many hunters, and they will hunt them down on every mountain and hill and from the crevices of the rocks"* (Jer. 16:14–16).

And everyone who calls on the name of the L*ORD* *will be saved; for on Mount Zion and in Jerusalem there will be deliverance, as the* L*ORD* *has said, among the survivors whom the* L*ORD* *calls* (Joel 2:32).

The ransomed of the L*ORD* *will return. They will enter Zion with singing; everlasting joy will crown their heads. Gladness and joy will overtake them, and sorrow and sighing will flee away* (Is. 51:11).

For further information,
or to receive a complimentary
six-month subscription to the
Messianic Vision Newsletter,
write to:

Messianic Vision
P.O. Box 1918
Brunswick, Georgia 31521
912/265-2500